TEACHER'S

TIME MANAGEMENT

SURVIVAL KIT

Ready-to-Use
Techniques and Materials

P. SUSAN MAMCHAK / STEVEN R. MAMCHAK

PARKER PUBLISHING COMPANY
West Nyack, New York 10994

Library of Congress Cataloging-in-Publication Data

Mamchak, P. Susan [date].
    Teacher's time management survival kit: ready-to-use techniques and
materials / P. Susan Mamchak and Steven R. Mamchak.
        p.   cm.
    Includes index.
    ISBN 0-13-014374-X
    1. Teachers—United States—Time management—Handbooks, manuals,
etc.   2. Classroom management—United States—Handbooks, manuals,
etc.   I. Mamchak, Steven R.   II. Title.
LB2838.8.M36   1993   93-373
371.1'024—dc20   CIP

Printed in the United States of America

10   9   8   7

ISBN 0-13-014374-X

PARKER PUBLISHING COMPANY
West Nyack, New York 10994

On the World Wide Web at http://www.phdirect.com

ACKNOWLEDGMENTS

We gratefully acknowledge the following educators whose determination and dedication have helped to produce this book. Thank you for sharing. Thank you for being so innovative and clever. For the thousands of students who have passed through your classrooms and have been so much the better for it, thank you for caring. And thank you for so freely sharing your love.

Evelyn Allaire
Tanya Ashuk
Clair Bailey
Fred Ball
Connie Barber
Roberta Bender
Kathy Brazas
Joseph Cole
Marci Crowe
Marshall Culver
Everett Curry
Walter Curry
Barbara Dean
Mark DeMario
Joan Dilger
Carole DiSalvo
Penny Divis
Elaine Douglas
John Dowling
Lisa Downs
Georgia Doyle
Buddy Ellison
Dorothy Feneshel
Sue Fream
Marilyn Freedman
Ron Gasparini
Fred Gernsbeck
Alma Gettings
Joseph Giamo
Marcia Giger
Howard Godfrey
Lynn Godfrey
Ed Golubinski
Kevin Graham

Warren Griffith
Ruth Griffiths
Barbara Gunther
Carol Hertgen
Auggie Hertzeg
Patrick Houston
Barbara Howard
Walter Hughes
Johnnie Johnson
Robert Johnson
Shirley Johnson
Rosemary Knawa
Phoebe Koontz
Don Kurz
Elaine Langer
Anita Laughton
Paul Lefever
Gloria Lehman
Patrick Leone
Lenore Marcelli
Sandy McCray
Betty McElmon
Ginny Mendes
Gary Meyerson
Maureen Mulholland
Joanna Neuenhaus
Andrew Newfeld
Ruth North
Al Olsen
Ruth Olsen
Ingrid Pedersen
Ron Pietkiewicz
Amy Pomerantz
Ruth Rechtin

Dolores Recupero
Eber Reitzel
Frank Reitzel
Diane Rodgers
Joey Ruggiero
Mike Ruggiero
Lynne Rubin
George Saffa
Ruth Scattergood
Bernhardt Schneider
Ginny Schwartz
Ida Sciala
Mark Sessa
Sol Shuck
Dan Sorkowicz
Janet Spears
Millie Stanton
Victoria Taylor
Olivia Thompson
Edith Tuffiash
Myron Turner
Ruth Underhill
Ed Van Houten
Shirley Van Zandt
Fred Vezzosi
Lynn Villa
Herbert Waters
Cynthia Wendell
Leonard Williams
Lynn Williams
Justine Wilson
Ed Zielinski

ABOUT THE AUTHORS

P. SUSAN MAMCHAK has served in many different educational posts, from substitute teacher to school disciplinarian to curriculum designer. She has also conducted workshops on teacher effectiveness, is a past member of Toastmistress International, and travels and lectures extensively. With her husband of 28 years, she is co-author of over a dozen books on education.

STEVEN R. MAMCHAK has been actively involved in education for over 30 years. He has worked with "disaffected" children as well as gifted and talented students, has hosted a weekly radio program on education, and is a frequent speaker to both educational and civic groups.

INTRODUCTION: ENHANCING YOUR TEACHING WITH TIME-SAVING TECHNIQUES

No one has to tell us that teachers work hard. We know that fact by the feeling deep inside when that final bell rings and the students erupt from the building. We know it by the realization that there remains for us the time we will spend correcting student papers, preparing tomorrow's classes, researching material for the next unit, and doing the many tasks that go into the activity that constitutes the major component of our lives—teaching.

Yet, as anyone who has taught for any length of time will tell you, that is just a part of it. As one teacher observed, "If all I had to do was teach, I'd think I'd gone to Paradise!" Of course, we know only too well the frustration that statement reflects, for teaching is often fraught with situations that place instruction on the back burners while we deal with the pot that boils over before our very eyes.

In the middle of your most intense teaching, the loudspeaker interrupts to announce Student Council election results, and the class explodes with a heated reaction that you will have to cool before instruction can continue. Everyone has settled down and the lesson begins when in comes a tardy student for whom you will have to stop teaching to handle. Several students raise their hands, and you know that they are going to ask questions, which you will be answering in a few moments, if only they wouldn't interrupt now. Billy is disturbing the class again, and you'll have to stop and get him settled before you can teach. Everywhere you turn, there are distractions that chip away at your precious teaching time.

Nor are students the only offenders. The principal needs you to supply figures for a report by 2 o'clock this afternoon. A parent has asked you to call, and you know from experience that she likes to talk and talk and talk. Lesson plans for next week are due before you leave today. The cafeteria wants that count of "A" and "B" lunches—and weren't you supposed to take your class down to the assembly program ten minutes ago?

The list seems to stretch on into eternity. If we listen closely, we can hear our fellow teachers sighing, "So much to do, so little time!"

If only there were a way to effectively capture the "time tiger" and pull its fangs. Every teacher longs for methods that allow for time-consuming tasks to be handled quickly and efficiently, freeing teacher time for what must be considered most essential—teaching itself. If only ways could be found to accomplish the goal of getting the time-wasting tasks taken care of to everyone's satisfaction while allowing teaching—*real* teaching—to continue without significant interruption.

Fortunately, because the abuse of time is a problem common to *all* teachers, the solutions that neutralize the "time acid" are universal as well. There *are* solutions that have worked effectively for other teachers; they *will work* for you!

What if we told you that there was a way (*see* "U Choose") to *cut the time spent in correcting compositions by one-half to two-thirds*? What if you knew that there was a method (*see* "Minimessage") that absolutely *stopped misbehavior without any interruption of teaching*? How about a way (*see* "Countdown") to ensure that *the phone call to that chatty parent covers all bases and lasts no more than ten minutes—guaranteed*? On the first day of class, would you want a way (*see* "Locator"), to establish a seating plan, assign lockers, pass out school materials, give out textbooks and begin instruction—*all in less than five minutes*? These are *not* fantasies dreamed up by a well-intentioned but totally impractical theorist. These are actual techniques found wiithin the pages of this book—techniques that have been *used in the classrooms of America*, have worked exceedingly well for other teachers, and *will work for you*!

Teacher's Time Management Survival Kit presents you with a treasure chest of practical, usable time management techniques that you *can and will use in your classroom*. It may involve taking instant attendance on a class trip (*see* "Bus Bingo"), ending a fight and effectively dealing with the combatants without significant interruption to the rest of the class (*see* "Your Side, My Side"), involving the home in the positive reinforcement of a student in a matter of seconds (*see*: "Chronicle"), instantly increasing the homework productivity of your students while saving your own valuable time (*see* "The Homework Calendar"), or cutting in half the time you must spend with sales representatives (*see* "Agenda One"). Whatever your need, we feel certain that you will find something that stands ready to meet that need with effectiveness and dispatch.

All the techniques have been crafted *by* classroom teachers *for* classroom teachers. All of the strategies are aimed at saving your invaluable time while handling the situation in the most efficient and practical manner possible. All of the methods are workable and will work for you.

Read about it this morning. Perhaps take it to the copier at lunchtime. *Use it in your classroom* this afternoon. Use it to handle those petty distractions to maximize your teaching time. Use it to manage your time more efficiently and effectively to the ultimate benefit of your students. Use it to free yourself from the routine in order to glory in the pure joy of teaching and helping children grow!

What are we waiting for? Time doesn't stop for us; we have to grab hold of it.

Let's get started!

P. Susan Mamchak
Steven R. Mamchak

CONTENTS

Applying School Rules to the Classroom (2) • Pre-empting Students' Premature Questions (2) • Handling Misbehavior During Instruction (I) (3) • Handling Misbehavior During Instruction (II) (4) • The Fighting Student (4) • The Rebellious Student (5) • The Academically Unprepared Student (6) • Effecting Smooth Transitions in the Classroom (6) • Quieting the Class Quickly (7) • Returning Borrowed Materials (8) • Dealing With Cleanliness in the Classroom (9) • Working With the Talkative and/or Disruptive Student (9) • Getting Back to Instruction Following a Disruptive Incident (I) (11) • Getting Back to Instruction Following a Disruptive Incident (II) (12) • Dealing With the Serious and Prolonged Behavioral Problem (13)

Reproducible Time Savers

SECTION TWO: HANDLING STUDENT HOMEWORK EFFECTIVELY 24

Reproducible Time Savers

SECTION THREE: RAPID AND EFFICIENT COMMUNICATION 47

Emergency Communications (58) • Handling Those Common Requests (59)

Reproducible Time Savers

SECTION FOUR: ENHANCING YOUR RECORDKEEPING EFFICIENCY 73

Handling the First-Day-of-School Information (73) • Obtaining Student Personal Data (74) • Effectively Keeping Textbook Records (74) • Handling Class Attendance Records (75) • Handling School Attendance Records (76) • Recording Quiz and Test Scores (76) • Using Student Aides for Recordkeeping (77) • Taking a Count for Class or School Records (78) • Taking a Lunch Count (79) • Collecting Money (I) (79) • Collecting Money (II) (80) • The Classroom Inventory (I) (81) • The Classroom Inventory (II) (81) • Locating Records When Needed (82) • Recordkeeping Checklist (83)

Reproducible Time Savers

SECTION FIVE: MANAGING STUDENT/TEACHER INTERACTIONS   96

Dealing With the Total Paper Load (I) (97) • Dealing With the Total
Paper Load (II) (98) • Correcting of Student Written Work (I) (98)
• Correcting of Student Written Work (II) (99) • Avoiding Arguments
Over Poor Grades (100) • Choosing Students to Work in Groups (100)
• Choosing Students to Answer Questions (101) • Avoiding Gender
Bias (102) • The First Day of the Subject (103) • Getting the Most
Out of Detention (104) • Supervising the Playground (105) • Working
in an Extracurricular Activity (105) • Talking with Students (106)
• Assessing Needs for Interaction (107) • Teacher Time-Management
Calendar (108)

Reproducible Time Savers

SECTION SIX: SAVING TIME IN YOUR ADMINISTRATIVE DUTIES   122

Getting the Most out of Faculty and Departmental Meetings (123)
• Dealing with the Total Mail Load (123) • Dealing with Advertising
Brochures (124) • Passing Out Flyers and Brochures (125) •
Evaluating Materials for Future Use/Purchase (125) • Working with the
Classroom Budget (126) • Meeting with Sales Representatives (127)

Reproducible Time Savers

SECTION SEVEN: LARGE AND SMALL GROUP MANAGEMENT

Reproducible Time Savers

SECTION EIGHT: MANAGING CLASSROOM ROUTINE   164

Those Opening Exercises (165) • Writing on the Blackboard (166) • The Hall Pass (166) • Passes to the Lavatory (167) • The Visitor in the Classroom (168) • Emergency Preparedness (168) • The Fire Drill (169) • Students Who Are Missing Worksheets (170) • The Learning Materials Trust Fund (170) • Students Without Learning Materials (171) • Bulletin Board Management (I) (172) • Bulletin Board Management (II) (172) • Keeping Textbooks in Reasonably Good Shape (173) • Assessing Textbook Condition (174) • Checklist for Routine Management (174)

Reproducible Time Savers

SECTION NINE: TIME-SAVING STEPS IN HOME-SCHOOL COOPERATION   185

Positive Parental Contact (I) (186) • Positive Parental Contact (II) (186) • Positive Parental Contact (III) (187) • Parental Contact Recordkeeping (188) • Involving Guidance In Parental Contact (188) • The Note or Item Sent Home (189) • The Note or Item Unreturned (189) • Getting a Handle on Parental Phone Calls (190) • Management of Parental Conferences (I) (191) • Management of Parental Conferences (II) (191) • Parent-Teacher-Student Cooperation (I) (192) • Parent-Teacher-Student Cooperation (II) (192) • Parents as Classroom Volunteers (193) • Keeping Parents Informed (194) • Checklist for Home Involvement (194)

Reproducible Time Savers

SECTION TEN: SAVING TIME IN SPECIAL SCHOOL SITUATIONS 206

The Class Party (I) (207) • The Class Party (II) (208) • The Class Play (208) • The Art Project in the Classroom (209) • Animals in the Classroom (210) • Using Movies/Video in Class (210) • Using the School Library (211) • Awards to Students (211) • Handling Special Gifts (212) • Going to that "Special" Assembly (213) • When Accidents Happen (213) • Sending Students to the Nurse (214) • Working with Computers (215) • The Teacher Evaluation (215) • Post-Evaluation Teacher Memorandum (216)

Reproducible Time Savers

BEFORE WE BEGIN

Let's start with an understanding. As teachers, we are dealing with people: children, teenagers, and perhaps even young adults. Each one is a unique individual, with unique talents, problems, and needs. We work with very precious, highly volatile, often unpredictable human beings. Consequently, what works for one, under one set of circumstances, may not necessarily meet the needs of another.

All of the time-saving techniques in this book have worked. None of them, however, is "chiselled in stone". None of them is so sacrosanct that it cannot be touched, reworked, adapted to special situations, and applied to *your* particular classroom or *your* peculiar circumstances. Indeed, adaptation, ingenuity, and the ability to change are hallmarks of good teaching and good teachers.

Every recipe in a cookbook has pleased somebody at some time. but that shouldn't stop you from adding an ingredient here and leaving out a spice there, until it appeals to your tast and the tastes of your families and friends to whom it will be served.

The analogy holds. The following pages contain receipes that have enjoyed success for many a "chef," but it is up to you to make each one uniquely your own.

Let's get started.

TIME MANAGEMENT
THROUGH EFFECTIVE DISCIPLINE

Teaching flourishes where there is order; it dies where chaos exists. In this section, we'll look at some time-saving strategies aimed at achieving and maintaining the discipline necessary to the learning process. From the application of school rules to your classroom, to dealing with the prolonged and serious behavioral problem, let's examine some ways in which educators have quickly and efficiently handled a variety of situations requiring discipline that most teachers face.

APPLYING SCHOOL RULES TO THE CLASSROOM

Has a student ever said to you, "I didn't know we had to do that!" or "I didn't understand that we weren't allowed to...?" You then have to take the time to go back over those rules, explain them and determine whether the child really didn't know or was merely trying to get out of trouble.

One of the best time-savers in these situations is to take away any excuse for *not* knowing the rules of the school as they apply in your classroom.

Schools generally give each student a handbook containing all the rules. If you take a close look at those rules, you will see that they can be reduced to four—yes, *four*—statements. We won't call them "rules;" we'll call them a "Student Success Code." You can see them in **Figure 1-1.**

First, make a really *large* copy of this figure. Make it so big that no one could possibly miss it. Post it prominently in your room, perhaps in the center of the bulletin board, with several smaller copies in plain view elsewhere. Let there be no place where these cannot be seen.

Now you are ready to use this to save time. If Philip comes without his notebook or text, have him read number two from the board; if Ellie doesn't have her homework, have her read number four; if Harry throws an object, have him read number three; if Tasha is tardy, have her recite number one. You can keep the student after school to explain a rule to you, do it on the spot, have the student write you a letter explaining the violated rule, or have a student explain a rule to his or her parents during a conference. The possibilities are endless.

Perhaps a student is prodding the back of the child in front of him. You knock on your desk, and when the boy looks up, you hold up three fingers and then point to the Student Success Code. The child looks, swallows hard, and goes back to his work.

Now, *that* is saving time!

PREEMPTING STUDENTS' PREMATURE QUESTIONS

Naturally, we want our students to ask questions. No teacher resents questions, but it can be extremely frustrating when you know that the questions being asked would be answered in a few minutes if only the students would allow the lesson to continue. There are times when you want your students to ask questions, and there are times when you want them to simply be quiet and listen.

One elementary teacher solved the problem with the poster in **Figure 1-2**. This shows the front and back of the same card. When the teacher is about to teach a new concept, she puts out the card with the "LISTEN" side showing. The children have been made to understand that now they are to *listen* and not ask questions. The lesson completed, the teacher turns the card to the "ASK" side and students are invited to ask whatever they would like.

A high school teacher uses the sign in **Figure 1-3**. The sign reads "Please ask" on one line and "QUESTIONS" on the line beneath. On a separate card he has printed "NO" on top and "NOW" on the bottom line. These line up with the words on the bigger sign. There are Velcro strips on the back of the smaller sign and in the appropriate places on the larger poster. When he wants a class without questions or interruptions, he presses the smaller sign into place, and it reads as in **Figure 1-3**. When the lesson is over, he removes the smaller sign, and it now reads, "Please ask QUESTIONS."

This "Word Approach" works better for the upper grades where happy faces might be considered childish.

This process must be clearly explained to the class. Never should they be made to feel that their questions are unimportant. They should be told why you are using this aid and that you will gladly welcome all of their questions once you have finished and the "Please ask QUESTIONS" side is showing. You might even suggest that they write down their questions so that they won't forget them when question time comes.

Once this has become an integral part of your classroom routine, it will save you a great deal of time and frustration.

HANDLING MISBEHAVIOR DURING INSTRUCTION (I)

Every teacher eventually comes up against a child who misbehaves during instruction. This is not only frustrating to the teacher, but it also robs the class of valuable teaching and learning time. Such behavior must be handled, however, or it will only become worse and take even more time away from learning.

In this and the following technique we'll look at two methods for handling minor misbehavior during instruction. This technique works best in elementary school, while the next seems to work better in secondary school.

Look at **Figure 1-4**. This was originally produced on a 3×5-inch index card. Several were made and kept in the teacher's desk. Suppose you are teaching, and you notice Martin busily making spitballs. You go to your desk as you continue teaching, remove one of the cards, and make your way to Martin's desk. Without a word to Martin or a second lost from instruction, you place the card on his desk and walk away.

That's it. Time lost from instruction is zero. Now, however, Martin has more to think about than spitballs. Since he must return the card to you at the end of the period, he has matter for mature reflection, and it should make him reappraise his spitball manufacturing, at least for the time being.

When the card is returned, it will be your judgment that determines what further action, if any, is required.

This works well for upper elementary and middle school.

HANDLING MISBEHAVIOR DURING INSTRUCTION (II)

In the secondary school, the problem remains the same, but the approach to the solution must be a bit more circumspect. If secondary students resent anything, it is being treated as children.

One high school teacher contends that the older the students, the more you must appeal to logic. She explains to her class that any student who would deprive the rest of the class from learning time is analogous to someone who would keep a hungry man from food. Therefore, anyone who would keep the class from learning should do something to compensate for the time lost. Is that not logical?

If, for example, there are 27 students in the room, and a student took two minutes away from the class through inappropriate behavior, is it not logical that the student now owes the class 2×27 (or 54) minutes of time?

How should the student repay the time? Possibilities include tutoring, heading a clean-up committee, making a new bulletin board display, or whatever else the teacher's knowledge of that student might dictate.

The first time a student misbehaves, the teacher places the person's name on the board, and no other action is taken. The next time during the same class, the teacher places next to the name the time in minutes she figures is going to be needed should she have to stop. The third time it happens, the teacher stops instruction, speaks to the offender, and places the times sign and the number of students in the class. At this point the student owes the class the indicated time. **Figure 1-5** shows the process as it might be written for a particular student.

Actually, this teacher informs us that she rarely gets to the third stage. Once introduced and reinforced, the mere writing of a student's name on the chalkboard is often enough to end the distracting behavior, sometimes even with a short, "Sorry!" from the student.

Virtually no time is lost with this method, and it does have the advantage of being logical and well-adapted to a secondary classroom.

THE FIGHTING STUDENT

There are few teachers who can get through the school year without witnessing at least one fight. If that conflict is of the "knock-down-and-drag-out" variety, then you will follow whatever policy your school dictates for the stopping and handling of it. If, however, it is a minor tussel, perhaps a war of hurled insults and "colorful" language, you might want to handle it yourself, particularly if it takes place in your classroom. If it does occur in your class, however, the difficulty is that the time taken to handle the situation is time taken away from your class and the lesson at hand.

One teacher solved that problem by formulating the sheet in **Figure 1-6**.

Whenever a minor "scrap" occurs, the students involved are separated and sent to desks at the opposite ends of the room. Each is handed the sheet in **Figure 1-6**. They are to fill it out completely, and they are to do it *now*! They sit and write while the class continues its work and you continue your teaching. When each has finished, you collect the paper and give it to the other combatant with the requirement that the student do what is indicated at the bottom.

Invariably, this process takes all period. In this time, both parties have had a chance to "cool off," the situation is defused, and you have had an opportunity to assess the situation and decide how next to proceed. Here, your knowledge of the needs of the students involved will determine future action.

Throughout, there has been precious little time lost or interruption of learning in the classroom.

Make several copies and keep them handy for use. Unfortunately, you probably won't have to wait very long to try them out.

THE REBELLIOUS STUDENT

Few students give us more problems than the "rebellious" student. This is the student who, by bearing, attitude, and action, seems to state, "I won't! You can't make me! I'll do what I want to do when I want to do it! I will not do what you tell me to do!"

We doubt that there is a teacher anywhere who can claim to have the solution to every rebellious student. Indeed, what works for one may not work for another. It is often frustrating and always time-consuming working with this student.

One of the few things that seems to work more often than it fails is the use of the student/teacher contract. Now, volumes have been written about the use of the contract in education, and it is not our purpose to go into that here. Rather, let us share with you a contract form that has worked.

Figure 1-7 is an example of an all-purpose contract. Make certain that it is for a short enough period of time to be attainable. Keep the expectations reasonable and geared to the individual student. Keep the penalties reasonable as well.

Keep it short, to the point, clearly understandable, and specify a short time for the first contract with ensuing longer times as future contracts are needed. If you start by requiring the child to "be good" for the next six months, the contract won't last the day. Start with a contract for a week or less, increasing or decreasing it as you witness the student's self-control develop or ebb away.

If the contract is successful, it can save you much valuable class time as well as bringing about some positive changes in the "rebellious" student.

Think of this as one more tool to save time and help a student who needs to be reached.

THE ACADEMICALLY UNPREPARED STUDENT

If today's lesson is built on last night's assignment, and Maria didn't do the assignment or study as directed, then Maria is behind the moment she sets foot through the door. Moreover, you are going to be spending a lot of time with Maria trying to bring her up to par with the rest of the class. The academically unprepared student poses a real problem.

One teacher approached this problem by informing his class that if a student came academically unprepared, not only would the student receive a negative grade for the day but would be expected to make up the work at the teacher's convenience. If, however, the unprepared student told the teacher *before* class that he or she was unprepared, the student would not be called on, no negative grade would be given, and the student could make up the work as he or she chose, as long as it was reasonable. These were the advantages of telling the truth.

When the student came to inform the teacher, however, he or she was given the card in **Figure 1-8**. The student filled in his or her name and the teacher filled in the rest. Since all this had to happen *before* class, there was no interruption of teaching. The teacher kept the card.

With the third occurrence came a penalty, and the student was now assigned a special make-up assignment. This, of course, is left to the teacher's discretion, since each student is an individual, and the teacher best knows that student's needs.

Once this system has been established in a class, and the students are aware that you are holding to it, experience has shown that fewer students come to class unprepared. Perhaps students come to the realization that the teacher is not about to let them *not* learn.

We think you will be satisfied with the time saved and with how the approach encourages more and more students to be academically prepared for class.

EFFECTING SMOOTH TRANSITIONS IN THE CLASSROOM

Teaching a class consists of many activities. There may be lecture, group work, reading, discussion, seat work, work on the chalkboard, a question-and-answer period, and more. Sometimes, effecting a smooth transition from one activity to another can pose a problem.

It is frustrating and often time-consuming to stop one activity and begin another, only to find that one student is still writing and another isn't ready because he or she is still getting books put away and getting ready for the activity that started several moments ago.

Several elementary teachers we know solve this problem by giving the class tangible sign to remind them that one activity must cease and another begin. One teacher claps her hands, says "Look!" and places a placard on the chalkboard edge. A flurry of activity begins. Books are put away. New books are taken out. Notebooks appear and are opened. Pencils become poised in hands. By the time the teacher has stepped to the front of the room, the class is entirely prepared for the new activity. That's a smooth and time-saving transition.

Figure 1-9 shows several examples of drawings that might appear on the placard. Once the children have been trained to recognize the meaning, a flag straight up could mean continuing with the present activity, and when it is turned over, the students should prepare for what is to come next (**A**). The same strategy could be applied to free time and time when they must quiet down (**B**). Students continue writing when the address side of an envelope shows but put away their writing materials when the flap side is displayed (**C**). This approach might also be used to differentiate between a writing and a reading period (**D**). Even two identical flowers (**E**), one white and the other red could be used to show the end of one activity and the beginning of another.

How effective this is as a time-saver depends on the use you make of it in your class. If you take the time to train the class, then you will find that they really do save time and make for smooth transitions. After the first month of school, you can get their attention and point to the card you've just put out. By the time you have your materials together for the next activity, your class will be ready too. That's smooth!

QUIETING THE CLASS QUICKLY

There are times when you want your students to interact, and that includes being noisy and talkative—sometimes. The problem comes along when you want them to cease talking and being noisy, and quiet down for the next activity. It is not that the teacher cannot quiet the class; it is just that it often takes an inordinate amount of time and energy to do so.

There is an easier and faster way for you and your class. Don't do it yourself; let kids quiet kids.

In many classrooms desks are arranged in rows (see **Figure 1-10**). The last person in each row (indicated by the *X*) is designated as a "quieter." When the teacher signals that person, that student gets up and proceeds to the person in front of him or her, telling that person to put things away and quiet down. The "quieter" then proceeds to the next desk and the next (see the pointers in **Figure 1-10**), repeating the message. When the "quieter" gets to the front of the row, he or she turns around and starts back down the aisle, reinforcing the message once more. By the time the "quieter" has reached his or her own seat, the teacher should be all ready to begin the new work.

Even if students are not in regular rows, this will still work. Let's say that students were working in groups with desks pulled together. All the teacher need do is contact the "quieters" and have them move about the class swiftly telling students to stop the present activity and get their seats and materials ready for what is about to happen.

This works because the students understand that the "quieters" are speaking for the teacher and that the teacher's authority stands behind the request to quiet down. Certainly, you will need to support these "quieters," especially during the first weeks when this technique is in operation.

Once established, however, the system saves you lots of time and trouble. When you want the class quieted, you inform your key students and they begin to move about the class, getting students to put away materials, sit down or quiet down, and generally restoring a receptive attitude to the class. When you are ready, you thank them, thank the class for their cooperation, and continue with the next lesson, all without any substantial disruption and in a relatively short period of time.

RETURNING BORROWED MATERIALS

Have you ever lent students books, erasers, pens or pencils, only to have them be gone forever? Isn't that frustrating and time-consuming? Certainly, we would like to accommodate the child who may have forgotten an article. But remembering who took what and then going after the child at the end of the class can tax your memory and use up time that might well be better spent.

One way to solve that problem is to use the slip in **Figure 1-11**. When a student comes to the desk asking to borrow anything, the child must first fill out this short form. The article is lent to the student, and this sheet is placed conspicuously on the teacher's desk. This might be on a message holder or clipped to the desk calendar, as long as it is someplace where the teacher can readily see it. The class continues as normal until the final bell.

When the student returns the item at the end of class, the sheet is either given to the student or torn up and discarded. If the item is not returned, you have the slip and can nudge the student's memory perhaps before the child leaves the room. If not, the slip is a reminder for tomorrow. If the student has lost the item, the slip is proof positive that the student needs to replace it.

An alternative to this method is to have the borrower leave something personal as "security" for the borrowed item. If Luis wants to borrow a pencil, perhaps Luis should leave his wrist watch on your desk. When he returns the pencil, he can retrieve the watch. Just make certain that the "security deposit" is of enough value to the student that he or she will want to get it back and thus return the borrowed item.

A math teacher we know found an excellent solution. A student who wants to borrow an item in her class must leave his or her *shoe* as collateral. Granted, she may have had a class of one-shoed students with which to deal, but she assures us that there has *never* been a case of a student failing to return a borrowed article since she began this practice. The only problem she reports is that the process gained such wide student acceptance that many of them were purposely leaving articles home, just so that they could go shoeless through the period!

It is understood that teachers who lend materials indiscriminately soon find themselves extremely low on supplies or running around the building trying to get things back from students who borrowed and then "forgot" to return them. That is not only a time-waster but a major inconvenience as well.

DEALING WITH CLEANLINESS IN THE CLASSROOM

Children are going to be children, and children often leave a mess. If they pick up the mess they make, all is well, but, realistically, they do not clean up automatically. Indeed, a teacher can spend quite some time seeing to it that scraps and papers are picked up, books are not left behind under desks, and that surfaces are free of graffiti, telephone numbers and messages written in assorted markers. You can spend a lot of time trying to keep your classroom clean.

One teacher solved the problem by initiating a system of desk and rows monitors. **Figure 1-12** shows the responsibilities each student has. This sheet was given to each monitor in order that full responsibilities would be clearly understood.

Before the period begins, *pre-monitors* check the condition of their rows and the desktops in their rows. If they find anything amiss, they report it to the row or desk monitor who records it for later reference.

When the class ends, the row and desk monitors do their check. If they find something on the floor or under a desk, they politely ask the student to pick it up; if they find writing on a desk that wasn't there at the beginning, they ask the student to remove it. When the class leaves the room, that room is clean and waiting for the next group.

If a student refuses to obey a monitor, he or she is reported to the teacher, who must handle each case individually according to that teacher's knowledge of the student involved.

Once this system has been established and reinforced, the students just accept it as another part of the classroom routine, and there is very little trouble from it. For upper elementary and middle school, this works really well.

This is an activity that will save you a great deal of time while actually improving the atmosphere of your classroom. You literally have the time from bell to bell to teach, without having to supervise tossed paper or messy desks. It instills good habits in your students, and it frees you to concentrate on your teaching.

WORKING WITH THE TALKATIVE AND/OR DISRUPTIVE STUDENT

By describing a student as "talkative" and/or "disruptive," we are not referring to the serious and prolonged behavioral problem. (We'll get to that.) Rather, this is the student who simply cannot or will not keep quiet or cannot or will not keep still. This student talks throughout the lesson, places that rubber spider on another student's desk, makes "funny faces" when your back is turned, eats away at your teaching time and the class's learning time.

You cannot ignore this student, for problems, and particularly behavioral problems, tend to proliferate if left to themselves. You cannot, however, spend the majority of class time dealing with this one student. The talkative and/or disruptive student poses quite a puzzle.

Let's investigate a method that has been used successfully in a number of classrooms in dealing with this particular student.

First, change the child's seat.   Place the child where he or she is within your view most of the time. Deny the student the privacy he or she needs to misbehave. Never place this child in a seat where he or she can "hide" and go unnoticed by the teacher.

Next, involve the child's home.   If moving the seat does nothing, call home. This procedure is often the most overlooked technique in all teaching. Certainly, there is the possibility of resistance from the parents, but in the vast majority of cases to which we have been a part, behavior significantly improved following the home contact.

Then, invite the parent(s) to monitor a class.   Arrange for one or both parents to come to school one day and sit in on their child's class. *But* don't tell the student they are coming. This is what makes it really effective. Think of the disruptive student coming into class to find Mom and Dad sitting silently in the back of the room. Imagine that you don't know when it could happen again. It can really make you think!

Finally, arrange a two-for-one exchange of time.   The student is informed that for every minute of class time wasted or caused to be wasted, he or she owes you twice that amount in real time to be served at the discretion of the teacher. As we have detailed previously in this section, that might be after school, before school starts, during recess, or any other time the *teacher* finds convenient. Don't make it easy for the child; you are trying to teach a lesson that the student will need in life.

One further action makes these four steps effective.

Throughout the process, inform the student of the next step to be taken; tell the student when you have taken the step; make the student understand that each step is occasioned by his or her behavior.   For example, tell the student that if the behavior doesn't stop, his or her seat will be changed. Change the seat to one close to you and say, "I have moved your seat, because you forced me to by not allowing the class to continue. If this doesn't work, I will have to call your parents." Let's say it doesn't work. You call the parents and tell the child, "An hour ago I called your mother and father and told them about your behavior. What you have been doing in class has forced me to do this. They want to speak to you, and if your behavior doesn't improve, you will force me to bring them to school to watch you for a period to see if we can understand why you behave the way you do." We have seen this work extremely well all the way through middle school.

You get the idea. The child is responsible for the consequences of his or her own actions and is made to recognize this. If you follow this procedure and apply it consistently, there will be a behavioral change for the better in all but the most hardened cases.

We have recapped the steps in the process in **Figure 1-13**. If you don't have to spend the majority of the class dealing with this type of behavior problem, then the time saved will be well worth your effort.

GETTING BACK TO INSTRUCTION FOLLOWING A DISRUPTIVE INCIDENT (I)

All of us have had our teaching disrupted at one time or another. There we are, in the middle of a super lesson, when something happens to bring it to a halt. The disturbance having passed, we are now faced with starting again, preferably at the point we left off.

We'll talk about the major disruption in the next section, but for now let's look at the minor annoyance that interrupts our teaching and eats up our time.

There goes the fire drill bell! You shout orders for windows to be closed and lights extinguished, as students scramble for the door and you search for your attendance book which isn't where you thought it was. Six minutes later, you are back in the classroom and anxious to get back to the lesson. "What page were we on?" asks one student. "May we open the windows?" chimes in another. "What book are we using? Is this in pencil or pen? Where were we? What are we doing?"

Of course, the miracle is that you *do* get back to instruction, but you pay a price for it, and that price is time and not a little bit of frustration.

A science teacher we know solved this problem by establishing a system that dealt with the unexpected. **Figure 1-14** is a form that this teacher passes out to his students. Not everyone would get one, just those students whose names are written in the blanks. Thereafter, those students are responsible for the various tasks outlined on the paper should an interruption of instruction occur. At the inception of the process, this teacher calls those students to his desk about once a week and goes over the tasks. After the process has been used successfully a few times, he informs us, they get the idea and remain conscientious in performing their assigned duties.

Let's take that fire drill. The bell rings and students go into action without having to be told. Windows are shut, lights turned off, shades drawn, page numbers recorded, and a mental note of what is being said is made. The students exit the room with you trailing, having found your attendance book.

Once back in the room, windows and shades are opened and redrawn as lights are turned on. The page number is written on the chalkboard for all to see. Finally, the teacher asks the assigned student to recap the lesson so far, including what materials were being used and what had been said or done. The teacher can get back into the lesson with an absolute minimum of distraction or lost time.

This technique was originally used with high school sophomores with great success. We see no reason why it could not be used throughout secondary schools and, perhaps with some modification in language and type of assignment, in elementary and middle school as well.

GETTING BACK TO INSTRUCTION FOLLOWING A DISRUPTIVE INCIDENT (II)

Now, let's talk about the major disruption: the child who "gets sick" all over another student; the major behavioral problem who must be removed from class; the announcement of the results of the cheerleading tryouts that have been awaited for days and days and days; the return to class following that *big* pep rally or that fantastic assembly where the magician sawed the principal in half! We'd call each of these a *major* disruption of instruction.

In these cases the aftereffects of the incident simply will not go away. A fire drill is soon faded from memory, but a class that is "hyped up" from the pep rally for tonight's big game is *not* about to quiet down quickly. The same is true if there has been an incident of illness in the room or if a student acted out so badly that he or she had to be ejected from the class. Your students are "keyed," and they will not simply forget it and return to normal.

In one successful method, the students are allowed to be excited and discuss the incident under controlled conditions, under the teacher's guidance, and for a specified period of time, after which all agree to return to instruction.

Let's take the pep rally. The class returns. They are sky high, shouting, cheering, voicing school slogans, and otherwise totally wrapped up in *the game!*

Don't say anything. Go to the chalkboard and write, "WHO WILL WIN TONIGHT'S GAME? WHY WILL WE WIN?" When the class has recognized the question, you will have gotten their attention. Now, *you* lead them in a discussion of the merits of your team. You guide them as they express themselves. You choose the people to talk. You run it as you would any class discussion.

Once it has gotten started, you can interrupt momentarily to set a time limit, let's say five minutes. Place the time the discussion will end on the chalkboard. A few times during the ensuing conversation, let the class know that the time is running down.

"There are about two minutes left," you might say. "Who would like to comment on what Yu-Lan just said?"

"That's it," you might conclude at the appointed time. "Time to get back to what this class is all about, but I want to thank you for this wonderful discussion. You know, you guys really can carry on a great conversation."

We once had a girl get "really sick" all over herself and the desks and materials within a couple feet of her desk. The girl having been sent to the nurse and the custodian notified, the class was moved to another room. They were flying high, and there were several unkind remarks about the girl who had taken ill.

On the board we wrote, "WHAT DOES IT FEEL LIKE TO BE EMBARRASSED?" The discussion stretched out to ten minutes, with several students sharing incidents where they had been terribly embarrassed by illness.

By the end of the discussion, not only was the class ready to return to instruction, but we had the definite feeling that when the girl returned to class, there would be no derision of her for the incident. Not only was the class able to get back to work, but perhaps they had learned a lesson that wasn't found in the textbook.

Try this method the next time there is a major disruption in your classroom routine. As long as *you* guide the discussion, you can keep it on track, establish a definite time for it to end, and spend a little time to save a great deal of time throughout the remainder of the period.

DEALING WITH THE SERIOUS AND PROLONGED BEHAVIORAL PROBLEM

The vast majority of the behavioral problems we face can be labeled minor, perhaps even petty inconveniences. Unfortunately, we also run into those that are truly deserving of the title "problem." We've taught a boy who enjoyed torturing smaller children with lit cigarettes, because he liked to hear them scream. We taught a boy who is currently serving a life sentence for rape and murder. We've dealt with drug dealers and drug abusers who sat in our classes. We worked with a girl who was into prostitution before she was 14.

Of course these are *not* representative of the majority of the kids we have taught. Nevertheless, they stick in your mind. You know the frustration you feel and the hours of time that you spend working such students.

There is a technique that will lessen your time and work. It does nothing to solve the serious behavioral problem, since solutions are as individual as the problems themselves, but it will be a tremendous help in dealing with the peripherals.

If a student with this serious a problem is in your class, he or she has probably come to the notice of the school authorities and those agencies developed to work with this student. If not, then that is your first line of action. In either case, the authorities—the Child Study Team, psychologist, guidance counselor—are going to come to you asking for a report or documentation of behavior.

The first time this happened to us, we spent hours prodding the corners of our minds, trying to remember incidents, trying to put them in chronological order, trying to prepare a coherent report that would be of value in handling this student.

Your answer lies in taking time in order to save time. If you have a serious behavioral problem in your class, go out and invest in a memo pad. On the inside of the top cover write the name of the student, your name, and the date begun. Thereafter, keep it in your desk. Place the current month at the top of the first page and wait. The first time and every time that the problem student does anything that is reflective of that serious behavioral problem, note the day and incident in that memo pad.

This is a typical sheet from such a pad. This one is fictional but reflects many an actual account. Use whatever shorthand you wish. "No HW, warned" obviously means that on the second of October, the student did not have homework and was warned about it. "Hit RG, rem. fr. cl." might mean to you that the student hit a boy named Robert Greene and had to be removed from class. So it goes. You are the one who is going to have to use it later.

If you were asked to give examples of poor behavior that you have personally witnessed, you are more than ready, not only with incidents, but with times, places, reactions, and what you did in the situation. You also have a verifiable, legal document that just might act as legal protection for you and that could stand up to challenge from virtually any quarter.

As we stated before, this won't solve the serious behavioral problem, but it will save you considerable time and effort, on all grade levels, while providing a solid basis for any commentary that may be required of you.

October
2 *No HW, warned*
3 *Hit RG, rem. fr. cl.*
4 *No HW, no cl. wk.*
5 *Fight w. JJ, removed*
6 *Throwing paper*

Student Success Code:

1. **Be Present and On Time.**

2. **Bring All Learning Materials With You.**

3. **Respect Other People and Their Property.**

4. **Be Prepared to Participate.**

Figure 1-1
Student Success Code

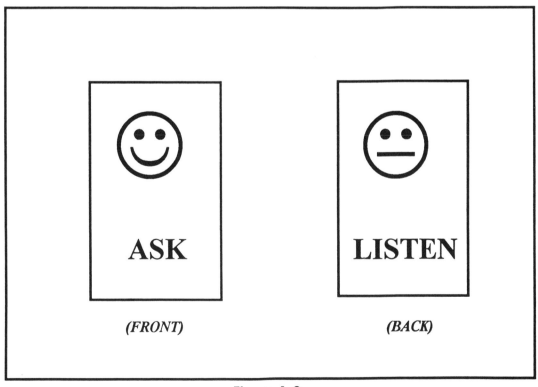

ASK

(FRONT)

LISTEN

(BACK)

Figure 1-2
Listen/Ask Card (1)

Please ask NO
_____
QUESTIONS NOW

Figure 1-3
Listen/Ask Card (II)

It looks to me as if you are disturbing the class.
This is unfair to me and the rest of the people in here.
 Please STOP right now. Bring this card to me at the end of the period.

Figure 1-4
Misbehavior Card

```
                                    # of students - 27
first offense:


        Rosemary

second offense:


        Rosemary   1

third offense:


        Rosemary   1 X 27
```

Figure 1-5
Misbehavior Time Card

Fill in this sheet COMPLETELY. Leave nothing out.

YOUR NAME: _____

TODAY'S DATE: _____   *PERIOD:* _____

With whom were you fighting? _____

Tell me your side. Use the back of this sheet if necessary:

_____

_____

_____

_____

_____

_____

_____

_____

_____

_____

_____

_____

_____

_____

_____

_____

_____

_____

_____

_____

_____

_____

_____

_____

_____

* *

To the other person involved — Read this and comment on the back of this sheet. Sign your name.

Figure 1-6
Student Fight Sheet

STUDENT CONTRACT FORM

Student's Name: _____

Contract to run FROM:_____ TO:_____

The STUDENT agrees to:

_____
_____
_____
_____
_____
_____
_____
_____
_____
_____
_____

The TEACHER agrees to:

_____
_____
_____
_____

If the STUDENT does not complete this contract, the
STUDENT agrees to:

_____
_____
_____

* * * * * * * * * * * * * * * * *

Date of Signing:_____
STUDENT'S Signature:_____
TEACHER'S Signature:_____
WITNESS:_____

Figure 1-7
Student Contract Form

NAME: _____

Date	Unprepared Assignment	Made Up
1.		
2.		
3.		

* *

When the above-named student has filled in this card (THREE UNPREPARED CLASSES), he/she agrees to do a special "make-up" assignment as directed by the teacher.

Figure 1-8
Unprepared Student Card

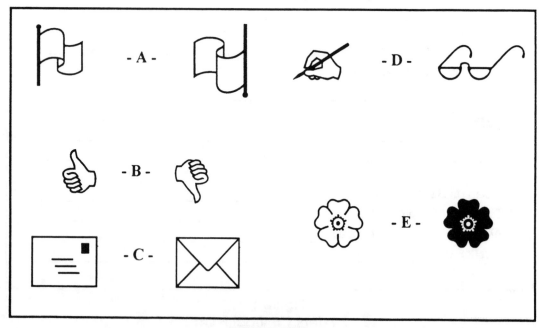

Figure 1-9
Changing Activity Pictures

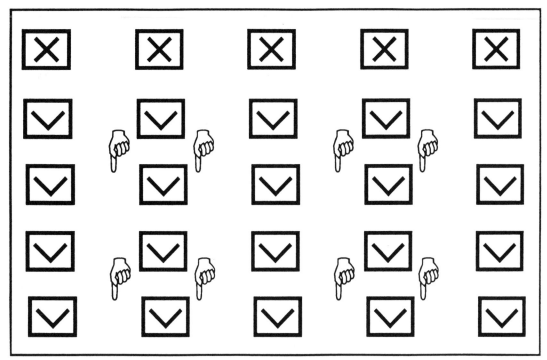

Figure 1-10
Quieting Class Diagram

BORROWING RECORD SLIP:

Name:_____

Date:_____ Period:_____

Item Borrowed:_____

Returned:_____

Figure 1-11
Borrowing Record Slip

RESPONSIBILITIES OF CLEAN-UP MONITORS

ROW PRE-MONITORS:	<u>Before</u> class begins, check your row for cleanliness and report anything unusual to the Row Monitor.
DESK PRE-MONITORS:	<u>Before</u> class begins, check the desktops in your row for cleanliness and report anything unusual to the Desk Monitor.
ROW MONITORS:	Check your row at the <u>end</u> of every class; look under each desk; politely ask students to pick up any refuse near or under their desks; if the row is not to your satisfaction, report it to the teacher.
DESK MONITORS:	Check the desktops in your row at the <u>end</u> of each class for writing, drawing, and/or marks of any kind; politely ask the student to remove the marks; if the desktops are not to your satisfaction, report it to the teacher
CHECKER:	Check everything <u>before</u> and <u>after</u> class.

Figure 1-12
Cleanliness Task Sheet

1. Change student's seat; deny student privacy for bad behavior.

2. Involve the home; make parent(s) aware of the situation; enlist their aid.

3. Invite parent(s) to come in to school to monitor their child's class; do not inform student beforehand.

4. Institute a policy wherein the student owes two minutes of his or her time for every minute of class time wasted due to bad behavior; this time to be spent at teacher's discretion and convenience.

THROUGHOUT: Inform student of next step in the process if behavior does not improve; inform student AFTER the next step has been taken; take every opportunity to allow student to see each step as a result of his or her own behavior.

Figure 1-13
Behavior Problem Progression Chart

EMERGENCY INTERRUPTION LIST:

Close and open windows:_____

Pull and adjust shades:_____

Turn out and on the lights:_____

Remember the page we are on
and write it on the board
following interruption:_____

Remember what was being taught
and give a short recap of it:_____

Take notice of and reset all
equipment in the room:_____

Figure 1-14
Emergency Interruption List

HANDLING STUDENT HOMEWORK EFFECTIVELY

Virtually all teachers recognize that homework is an important part of the learning process. Indeed, homework is here to stay. Unfortunately, so are problems with homework. From assigning homework to collecting and grading it, from the child who copies another student's work to the one who refuses to do any work at all, from the student who has to make up missed work to the student who really has trouble with the assignment—all are part of our daily routine as teachers.

Let's examine some techniques that have saved time for busy teachers, while handling some very common homework problems with efficiency and dispatch.

ASSIGNING STUDENT HOMEWORK (I)

Have you ever assigned homework to students who didn't write it down, who copied it on the palms of their hands, who scribbled it on a postage-sized scrap of paper? Have you had students tell you that they lost the assignment book, couldn't remember what to do, and no one else in class had it either?

One group of teachers solved these problems by coming up with a Homework Calendar reproduced in **Figure 2-1**. This is a full-size sheet of paper that has been divided into days and subjects, providing spaces for the recording of homework assignments in each subject, for each period, for a full week. When used properly, it is an enormous time-saver.

The five teachers who came up with this shared five classes in a cluster setup. On the first day of the week, the first period teacher passed out one of these to each student. The teachers further agreed among themselves to give the homework assignments for the entire week each Monday. Thereafter, the assignments were expected to be done without further reminders.

There was no stopping each day to make sure that the assignment was written down; one day per week took care of that. There were no excuses allowed, for even if a student had lost the sheet, there were some 28 or 29 other students who had *not* lost the sheet, who knew what was expected, and who could be contacted to get the assignment. Even had a student been absent on a given day, the telephone made it possible to get all the homework that had been assigned.

We are certain that you can see the time-saving benefits attendant to the Homework Calendar. Once this has become established as part of the routine of the group, the time, effort and frustration saved by its use are enormous. Moreover, this technique is effective on any grade level where homework is assigned on a regular basis.

It may be simple, but it really works!

ASSIGNING STUDENT HOMEWORK (II)

The previous technique dealt with the assignment of homework. Now let's look at a method for saving time in developing the homework to be assigned.

A student once told us, "You give us dumb things to do, and there's too much of it! You don't know what it's like to be a student!" Perhaps there was a grain of truth in that; so, after quite a bit of consideration, we established a Homework Brigade. Basically, for the next several weeks, we allowed the students to make up the homework that they and their classmates would have to do.

The Homework Brigade consisted of five students. On Thursday, they were told what we would be covering the following week (just refer to your planbook), and each student was given the task of coming up with the homework assignment for the specific lesson on a given day. Melinda, for example, would make up the homework for Unit Five, Lesson Six, The Direct Object, which would be covered next Wednesday.

We used an index card as in **Figure 2-2**. It was filled out by the student and returned, completed, the following day. At a glance you can see the student's name, the class for which the homework is intended, and the actual homework assignment.

Of course, some restrictions had to be applied. A student could not assign *no* homework, nor could an assignment consist of a one-problem or one-sentence exercise. The assignments these students prepared had to meet the same standards the teacher's assignments did. They had to be meaningful, they had to be reflective of the material taught, and they had to fit the school's policy for length of time spent on doing homework.

This type of student-generated homework would work well in a middle school or secondary school where students have gained some perspective on the issue. We have heard of it done on an elementary level, but much closer teacher supervision was required.

If possible, every student in the class should get a chance at making up a homework assignment. The class can gain insight into the educational process that they may not get elsewhere. Even now, we will walk into class and state, "Tonight, one of *you* is going to give the homework assignment."

We'll tell you this: They sure pay attention!

MAKING UP HOMEWORK AFTER STUDENT ABSENCE (I)

You are in the process of collecting homework when one or two students appear at your desk. "We were absent yesterday," they intone. "What are we supposed to do?" And, there you are, searching your planbook and waiting while the students copy down the assignments. Even if you've kept a separate record of homework, getting it to those students who have been absent can often steal valuable minutes from your class while distracting you from the lesson at hand.

One teacher saved herself a huge amount of time and handled the problem most efficiently in a manner that could be applied to almost any grade level where consistent homework is required.

One child in the class was appointed as the Absentee Student. It was this student's duty to be the keeper of the paper in **Figure 2-3**. Each day for a week at a time, this student recorded the name of any student who was absent, the date of the absence, and the assignment for that day. The paper was brought to the teacher at the end of class, and she kept it overnight. A record of the missed assignments, therefore, was always present in the room. The teacher also appointed an alternate for the Absentee Student, and if both were absent, the task was temporarily assigned to another present student.

When the missing students came back to class after an absence, it was the duty of the Absentee Student to go to them and inform them of the assignments that had been missed.

If any "special" circumstances were involved, the teacher could always step in and stop or amend the process. For the most part, however, the transfer of missed assignments due to absence was now handled in an efficient and time-saving manner for the teacher. Students could never use the excuse that they did not know what assignments had to be made up or that they were supposed to be made up.

It worked out well for this teacher, and it will be of value to you as well.

MAKING UP HOMEWORK AFTER STUDENT ABSENCE (II)

What do you do with the student who steadfastly refuses to make up the missed work, even after it has been given? The fact that the student knows what to do is no guarantee that he or she is going to rush home and do it. Certainly, if a teacher decides to go after the missing work, it can be a time-consuming process.

A middle school teacher uses an innovative technique that is designed to save time while handling this situation.

She uses the document in **Figure 2-4**. Essentially, it is a contract. Let's look at how it is used in practice.

Once informed that the work is due, the student is also required to fill out one of these sheets. The student fills out all but the bottom part. When it comes to the penalty part, the teacher prescribes one in keeping with the individual student and his or her needs. If the teacher always has the same penalty, it might be typed on the sheet. Perhaps, under guidance, the student might assess his or her own penalty. There are many possibilities.

After the student completes the sheet, you take it for safekeeping until the student hands in the work or until the due date comes and passes. Whichever happens, the teacher notches the appropriate box, signs and dates it, and places it in a file for possible future reference.

Notice that in all of this the responsibility has been shifted from the teacher to the student. There is written record that the student received the time and opportunity to make up the missed work. There is a record that the student did or did not fulfill the promise. Much has been accomplished by this simple technique.

Understandably, this technique works best in middle school and high school. It is worth a try in the elementary grades, but much more supervision would be required, and the contract would have to be amended to meet the needs of the younger children.

COLLECTING STUDENT HOMEWORK

"Should we put it on your desk? Do we give this to you? Where do you want this?" All this, screamed in the midst of mass confusion *could be* the result if you have not successfully organized the collection of student homework.

From a number of teachers we have garnered a three-step process for homework collection that saves time and really works well in handling this process.

First, establish a single process for doing it. You may have students place their homework on your desk as they enter or put them in a basket as they leave. Or you may establish a Homework Monitor who collects homework at the same time every day. Whatever your method, just be comfortable with it, establish it early in the school year and stick with it until it becomes an established part of classroom routine.

Second, place as much as possible in the hands of the students. Make the students responsible for the collection of homework, not the teacher. All of the techniques in the previous paragraph place the duty of handing in homework on the students. Don't go around collecting homework; let them come to you.

Finally, let there be no deviation from the process. If Maria and Bobby want to argue that they had the homework, but a dog attacked them and ate it on the way to school, they will have to do so *after* class. Class will *not* stop for three minutes while we argue about homework-eating dogs. Adopt an "either-you-have-it-or-you-don't" approach, and you will be pleasantly surprised by the amount of time this simple stratagem alone will save you.

Let us share one short homework collection system that really works well. One student in each row is appointed as Homework Monitor for that row and is given the sheet in **Figure 2-5**. The student fills in the names of the students in his or her row and then proceeds to collect homework from the children. As homework is or is not handed in, the monitor checks off the appropriate column. The monitor then takes the collected homework and places it on the teacher's desk with this sheet on top. Other monitors are doing the same thing.

In a remarkably short time, all homework is collected and on your desk. You also have a written, verifiable record of who did and did not turn in homework on a particular day. And there has been *no* interruption of teaching, *no* teacher frustration, and *no* loss of teacher time.

We have seen this technique work extremely well in the middle school, and we are assured that it works equally well in elementary and high school.

PROVIDING INCENTIVES FOR DOING HOMEWORK

There is not a teacher anywhere who has not had students who did not hand in homework or handed in partially done or very sloppy work. Trying to work with these students and staying on them to produce homework on a regular basis and up to their best ability can often be a time-consuming and thankless endeavor.

That's why a math teacher we know came up with The Homework Pass in **Figure 2-6**. As you can see, it would easily fit on a 3×5-inch index card. As you might expect from reading it, this card is used *in place of* one homework assignment. Let's see how it is used in class.

This math teacher gives homework every night. When an assignment is done and done properly, this is indicated on the child's paper and in the teacher's marking book. When a child has collected five such papers, he or she may come to the teacher, show the papers, and receive a Homework Pass. This pass may then be used at the student's discretion, immediately or at some future date.

To use the pass, students take a blank sheet of paper, place their name and other required information on it, indicate the assignment the pass is replacing, and staple the pass to the paper. This is handed in and recorded as homework having been done.

Remember, each Homework Pass used indicates that the student did *five* fully complete, thoroughly prepared homeworks.

This teacher indicated that she has seen a rise in the amount of homework turned in. This has saved her a great deal of time having to deal with students who are missing work, and, since she bases most of her quizzes and tests on homework assignments, it has meant a general increase in the overall performance of the class.

DEALING WITH THE MISSING HOMEWORK PAPER

Suppose a student maintains with great vehemence that he or she had the paper when class started, handed it in, and somewhere between his or her desk and the teacher's desk, it disappeared ... vanished ... went! The student has no idea what may have happened to it.

We cannot dismiss the situation out of hand, for certainly we must *be* fair if we are going to teach our students about fairness. Whether the child is lying or telling the truth, however, is a time-wasting situation where the class loses as student and teacher engage in endless dialog about the missing homework paper.

Here are three approaches to the problem.

We previously detailed a method whereby student monitors collected homework from the class while indicating who did and did not have it. If you use this technique, showing the collection record (see **Figure 2-5**) to the student and asking him or her to account for the discrepancy often settles the matter on the spot. In a situation like this, it saves a lot of time.

Another method might be to establish a student "homework checker" who receives the collected homework papers and does nothing more than check them against the class roster. Thereafter, the student might hand the teacher a note such as seen in **Figure 2-7**. In this case, before the class ended, the teacher would have a list of papers not handed in, and those students could be contacted as the teacher desired. If the student protested, the papers were there to look through.

Finally, you might ask the student to put it in writing and submit it to you for your consideration. Immediately, class time is no longer being taken, and we have seen the protests end at this point. If students actually write out their case, we would give them the benefit of the doubt, for rarely will students who are telling a tale go through this procedure to vindicate themselves.

Any of these methods would work well on any grade level where homework is an essential part of the class, from upper elementary through secondary classes.

Use the one that best suits you, your teaching style, and your class, and it should help you to effectively cope with this sometimes perplexing difficulty.

COPYING ANOTHER STUDENT'S HOMEWORK

Most of us have shared the experience of coming across a student who is diligently copying another student's homework. The assignment that the child didn't do may be for another teacher or for you, but the child is copying work *not* his or her own. The student is cheating.

In handling this problem, we must be aware that what the student is doing is wrong. It is stealing another person's property; it is a dishonest act. In dealing with the student, therefore, our goal should be rehabilitation rather than mere punishment.

Let's look at a three-step process that has worked to cut down on copying, handle the problem in a positive manner, and save time for the teacher.

First, the copying should be established beyond doubt. After that, both the copied paper and the paper given to be copied should be torn up and thrown away. Unless the provider of the paper did so under threat or physical fear, neither the copier nor the accessory should be exempted from blame.

Next, the copying student must be made to see that what he or she has done is wrong. Have the student tell you why cheating is wrong. Have him or her do research on the concept of "private property" and explain how it relates to the case at hand. Have the student take the teacher's point of view and explain in detail why cheating is not allowed in class. Your purpose is to make the students realize that what they have done is wrong, not just because they got caught, but because it is *wrong* to cheat or steal.

Finally, the student must make restitution. One approach would be to use the sheet in **Figure 2-8**, which leaves it to the student to determine the compensation for having copied another student's work. Of course, you will help guide that choice. Possibilities include doing double assignments for a specified time, giving up a recess or after-school time to help another student, taking down assignments and getting them to absent students, doing some general task to assist the teacher, giving a reduction in credit, or assigning detention. Naturally, you will suit this compensation to the needs of the student involved.

It is particularly important that a system such as this be used in the lower grades, well before middle school years, for we all know that the patterns of a lifetime are reinforced during this period.

If you are consistent with such a method, you will find yourself needing it less and less frequently, and that is to everyone's advantage—you and your students.

REFUSING TO DO OR HAND IN HOMEWORK

However much you try and whatever effort you put into it, sooner or later you are bound to come up against a child who refuses to do homework. We do not mean the child who occasionally doesn't hand in a homework paper. Rather, we are speaking of the child who consistently *refuses* to do *any* work.

The time and effort, not to mention the frustration, that this child can require of you are monumental. As teachers, we must try, however, for the potential benefit of this student.

We will assume that the homework assigned served a real purpose by contributing to the student's final grade or its use on tests and quizzes or its reinforcement of classroom learning. We will further assume that you have taken several steps to try to remedy the no-work situation, and these attempts have not met with success. The student continues to do nothing.

If this is true, then it stands to reason that you are dealing with the rebellious student as defined at length at the end of Section One. Although there have been turnabouts in behavior, the child who has reached this stage is either already getting professional help or should be swiftly and forcefully recommended for it. At this point you should start documenting the case in order to supply information and insight as may be required.

Toward that end, every time the student does *not* have his or her homework, have the student fill out the form in **Figure 2-9**. It is self-explanatory. This will provide you with a tangible record of undone assignments and a log of excuses or lack of them. Indeed, the "excuse" section may be left blank, as long as the student signs the sheet. If he or she refuses to sign, then you sign and indicate the reason, making certain that you date it.

What do you do with these besides keeping them as a record? Try copying them and sending them home. If your school sends out warning notices or progress reports, attach the copies to these sheets. Try to send it home by registered mail, return receipt requested, for obvious reasons.

If you or your school has a policy that lack of homework affects a student's final marking period grade (for example, five missing homeworks may lower a final average by one grade), then make certain that the parents and the student are aware of this. If possible, get them to sign a statement to that effect (see Figure 2-13). No one should be able to say that he or she didn't know what was going to happen in this matter.

If all this works, and the student begins doing the work, then it is time for rejoicing. If the student continues along the same, self-destructive path, at least you have focused the problem in the minds of the student and the parents, gotten a record indicating the severity of the problem and attempts made to remedy it, and produced some valuable insights for the Child Study Team or other agency to whom the child has been referred.

If this doesn't save you time, it will certainly save you trouble on all grade levels where this problem may exist.

GRADING OF STUDENT HOMEWORK (I)

If you are going to assign homework and hold students responsible for its completion, the least you can do is to mark the work and return it to the students. That seems reasonable and fair, and that is the way most teachers feel about it.

But if you teach five classes per day of between 27 and 30 students each, then you are grading between 135 and 150 papers per night. That's a heavy load!

Therefore, we will look at two methods of grading homework that can be real time-savers for a busy teacher.

Let's talk about a *three-check* system. A student or students collect the homework (See Figure 2-5), and if the student hands in a paper, the student aide places a check mark on the assignment. The papers then go to another student who checks to see that the entire assignment was done. If so, he or she places a second check mark on the paper. At this point, only papers with two check marks are corrected further. All others are incomplete assignments.

The third check may be added in a number of ways. If the answers are either right or wrong, a key given to another student might allow that student to correct the papers. Or papers may be redistributed to students, with no one having his or her own paper, and corrected in class as part of the lesson. You may also go over them with most of the routine matters already done, giving each a quick assessment. If the work measures up to standards set by you (such as 7 out of 10 correct, for example), a third check is added to the paper.

In recording the graded homework, you now have an easy way to assess each effort. It is either missing (no checks), present but incomplete (one check), present and complete but incorrect (two checks), or present and complete and correct (three checks). If you substitute the numbers 0, 1, 2 and 3 in your marking book, it will make averaging out a homework grade a relatively easy task.

Figure 2-10 sums up the entire procedure and it can act as a handy reference.

We have seen this work well in upper elementary and middle school grades, and it is certainly worth a try at the secondary level, but that would be up to you and your knowledge of your class.

GRADING OF STUDENT HOMEWORK (II)

Now let's look at another method that has been used successfully to save time in the grading of student homework.

Decades ago, when we first set foot in the classroom as teachers, other teachers were advising us to use student aides for some of the tasks of daily classroom life. One teacher even advised using students to correct tests and quizzes and homework. While we could see how this might be done when the answers were of the right-or-wrong variety, our objection came with those assignments where *degrees* of right and wrong are involved.

With that same thought in mind, one teacher developed the guideline in **Figure 2-11**. This teacher has students correct the majority of the homework with only special assignments corrected by him. This teacher gets student volunteers and spends an afternoon after school with them. In that session, he trains them to correct homework. As previously noted, the right-or-wrong variety pose no problem, and for those requiring some judgment, he has his students use the Grading Guide.

This guide is self-explanatory and is constructed so that the answer Yes is always an indicator of something positive. Students use this guide when required, and most of them have the thing memorized by the time they have gone through a set or more of homework.

Of course, if you want to try this, you should feel free to alter and amend those questions until they reflect what you desire your students to look for in the answers to your homework assignments. It should be personalized for you and your class.

GIVING BACK STUDENT HOMEWORK

So far in this section, we have spoken about assigning homework, getting kids to do it, collecting and even grading it. Now let's look at the process of handing back that homework to our students.

Our aim is to save time that we may devote to actual teaching while, in the same instance, effectively handling the necessities of classroom routine. Returning homework is a case in point.

In any classroom, you can spend a great deal of time engaged in the handing out or handing back of materials. It may be homework or a flyer from the PTA, but it will take time and effort on your part. But who said *you* had to hand things out? If you permitted someone else to do it, you would not have to waste the time. Furthermore, if it were handled quietly and efficiently, you could even be teaching while it was being done.

Let's look at two techniques that fill the bill.

First, try giving the corrected papers to one or two student aides to hand back. There should, however, be restrictions. These aides may be required to report to class a few seconds early, get the papers, and stand at either side of the door to the room, returning papers to students as they enter. This might take a few seconds longer than normal, but, once inside, everyone has his or her paper and you are ready to begin without a substantial disruption of your teaching time.

Or you might give the papers to student aides to pass out silently during class, with the stipulation that there is to be no calling out of names or tossing of papers, of course. Certainly, this could be done quietly enough to allow you to continue with the lesson.

Now let's look at a method where student aides are not used.

When homework is being collected, take the papers for a single row and place a paper clip on the bunch. If you have five rows in your classroom, you will have five bunches of homework papers. Keep these papers together when they are being corrected.

Before the class comes into the room, place these papers on a table or the top of a bookshelf that is convenient to all students as they enter. Lay them out in five piles, one for each row. As the students enter the room, they go to the pile for their row and extract their homework paper. Since there are only five or six people in a row, finding an individual paper should be a relatively short task.

Once the students have established this as part of the daily routine, it should go very quickly, and a great deal of time will be saved for the teacher and the class.

The first technique seems better suited to the upper elementary grades and the middle school, while the second method seems designed for the secondary setup where students have gained a relatively greater degree of maturity.

Whenever this much time can be saved by a simple expedient, it is certainly worth trying to see if it works for you.

CONTACTING THE HOME ABOUT HOMEWORK (I)

We all realize that during the course of the school year it may become necessary to contact a student's home for a variety of reasons. Unfortunately, most of that contact seems to be negative. We have a tendency to contact the home only when there is something wrong. Sometimes, the home does not react as we hope they will, and help is not forthcoming from that sector.

Look at it from the parents' point of view:

If all you heard was bad news, perhaps you'd be reluctant to respond as well. Indeed, if we are speaking of time-saving methods, then one method that will really save time is to put forth some effort when things are going well to ensure cooperation when they are not.

The card in **Figure 2-12** is an example of one method of contacting the home about homework in a positive method, thereby paving the road for cooperation should a problem arise in the future. As you can see, it is easily filled out and may be given to the student to take home. Notes of *this* type invariably do reach the home front.

Of course, you must set some criteria for the issuance of this note. You may wish it to be a month of solid, well-done homework, two weeks, a single week, or, if you were trying to encourage a particular student, even a few days.

This, as well as the exact wording of the note, is up to you, but we wish you would try this. It really does save time, in addition to building a positive relationship between home and school. Later, should a problem arise, a call home that might begin, "*We* have a problem . . ." could be the beginning of a solution that will save you time and frustration as well as helping your student.

Adapt the note in **Figure 2-12** to your circumstances and personality, your class, and the particular student in question. See if it does not make things a great deal easier for you in the long run.

We think you will be pleased with the results.

CONTACTING THE HOME ABOUT HOMEWORK (II)

The previous method is used when things are going well. Now let's look at a scenario in which a child is handing in homework only once or twice out of every five assignments. The work is sometimes there and sometimes not. There is no consistency.

If you have already contacted the home in a positive manner, this would be the time to enlist their help. But if you have not contacted the home, if the child never did anything positive enough for long enough to warrant the note in **Figure 2-12**, then what do you do?

Let's look at a good method for communicating negative news about homework.

Do you have a policy concerning homework? If you, your group, your department or your school has one, this is the place to start. If, for example, a part of that policy states that four undone homeworks equals a reduction in a marking period grade, then make the parents aware of this as early in the school year as possible. A statement of policy should be sent home to every parent or guardian, and there should be some return that indicates that the parents have read and understand the document. **Figure 2-13** is a simple example of something at the bottom of the statement for the parent to sign, detach and return via the child. These should be kept on file.

Now, faced with such a situation, you can enlist the aid of the parents. When the child has reached his or her fourth undone assignment (in our example), it is time to act. When the child has reached the stage where the undone homework could affect his or her marking period grade, the sheet in **Figure 2-14** is made out and sent home.

There should, of course, be some verification that it reached home. This might mean adding a verification slip like the one used in **Figure 2-13**, asking the student to sign a verification that he or she had been given the note to be delivered, or following up with a phone call (our favorite) a couple days later.

We have seen a single notice of this type bring about a complete turnaround in a student. In all honesty, we have also seen it have no effect at all. When it does work, however, the change is stunning, and this technique is good for all grade levels.

Let us emphasize again that if you have built rapport with the home through positive contact, then this notice is going to be very effective. Certainly, it can be used alone, and most of the time it gets results, but if a basis of positive interaction has been established with the home, they are infinitely more predisposed to cooperate and handle any negative situation that may arise.

CHECKING STUDENT PROGRESS IN HOMEWORK

To many students, homework is nothing more than an arduous task to be performed every night. It seems of little value and often appears to be completely divorced from what is taking place in school or on their report card. Not all students think this way, of course, and we, as teachers, certainly know better. But if enough students have this perception, it can become a real problem.

There are a number of ways in which we can allow our students to see the effect that homework has on their daily learning in school and their eventual grade. Make the assignment a part of the class, including some new learning that was part of the previous night's homework. Use questions from the homework for your quizzes. Allow homework questions to form a question pool from which you will develop the next unit test. Each time you cover something new, emphasize how it was covered in the homework you assigned. Post outstanding homework papers on the bulletin board. Praise well-done homework. Allow students to get started on assignments during the last few minutes of class. There are many possibilities.

One teacher allows students to see how homework affects their subject grade. She uses the grid in **Figure 2-15**. This is given to each student at the beginning of each marking period. When an assignment is given back, it is recorded on this sheet. This teacher uses the 0-3 marking system explained in "Grading of Student Homework" (page 32), and every student records the grade for every assignment given, even if it is "0." She will call a student or two to her desk and check this sheet every now and then to see that it is being done accurately and properly.

Directions for finding your own homework average are clearly stated, as is the policy regarding undone homework. Obviously, you can make this grid as long or as short as you wish.

This saves time in a number of ways. It stops all arguments almost before they've begun, since the evidence is so clearly stated and often a matter of pure math. It precludes any charges from the student about being uninformed. The teacher who does this reports that now she doesn't have as many students around her desk asking about their homework status or what does and does not need to be made up. Finally, it gives the conscientious students a chance to see their good efforts contribute to a good grade, while allowing the nonworking, nonproducing students to clearly see that they are totally responsible for the grades they receive.

This teacher also reports that referring to the grid during a conference with the student and parents has led many times to better and more frequent homework.

All of this can save time for the teacher while helping the student realize the merit of homework. It may not be a panacea, but it's worth a try.

A SPECIAL NOTE

All the techniques in this section are intended for use in a normal classroom setting with children from the general school population. Naturally, if a child *cannot* do the homework due to some special factor, the techniques may or may not work or may need to be adapted to the student's unique needs. In cases such as these, the teacher should consult the Learning Disabilities Specialist or the school's Child Study Team.

STUDENT HOMEWORK PLANNING CALENDAR

NAME:_____ for the week of_____

PERIOD	DAY OF THE WEEK				
	MON.	TUES.	WED.	THURS.	FRI.
1. Subj.					
2. Subj.					
3. Subj.					
4. Subj.					
5. Subj.					
6. Subj.					
7. Subj.					
8. Subj.					

Figure 2-1
Student Homework Planning Calendar

Name:_____

Class for which assignment is to be developed:_____
_____
_____
_____

Homework Assignment:_____
_____
_____
_____
_____

Date given:_____
Date due:_____

Figure 2-2
Homework Brigade Form

Subject:_____ Month:_____						
Student Absent:	Date of Absence and Assignment					

Figure 2-3
Absentee Student Record

HOMEWORK MAKEUP AGREEMENT

*Name:*_____ *Period:*_____
*Date(s) of Absence:*_____
*Date of Return:*_____ *Today's Date:*_____

Assignment(s) Missed:

_____
_____
_____
_____
_____

I agree to make up the assignment(s) by:

_____

I understand that if the work is not made up by the above date , the following action will be taken:

_____
_____
_____
_____

(   ) Work handed in on _____

(   ) Work not handed in by specified date.

*TEACHER:*_____ *DATE:*_____

Figure 2-4
Homework Makeup Agreement

ROW # _____ HOMEWORK MONITOR

Monitor:_____Date:_____

Student	Homework	YES	NO
_____	_____	( )	( )
		( )	( )
		( )	( )
		( )	( )
		( )	( )
		( )	( )
		( )	( )
		( )	( )

* *

Please hand in this sheet with collected homework.

Figure 2-5
Homework Collection Sheet

Homework Pass

**In Recognition of Work Well Done,
This Card May be Used in Place of
ONE Assigned Homework.**

Teacher:_____

Figure 2-6
Homework Pass

STUDENT CHECKER: _____

DATE:_____ PERIOD:_____

Missing Homework Papers

_____
_____
_____
_____
_____
_____
_____

Figure 2-7
Homework Collection Record

NAME:_____ DATE:_____

To help compensate for my action of: _____
_____

I agree to do the following:_____
_____
_____
_____

Figure 2-8
Student Restitution Sheet

NAME:_____ DATE:_____

SUBJECT:_____ PERIOD:_____

TEACHER: _____

I did not to the following assignment: _____

_____

It was due on: _____

I did not do the homework assignment because:_____

_____

_____

_____

_____

_____

I am responsible for this statement.

STUDENT'S SIGNATURE:_____

Figure 2-9
Homework Excuse Form

☐   **NO CHECKS (0): No Paper; Missing**

☑   **ONE CHECK (1): Handed In But Incomplete**

☑ ☑   **TWO CHECKS (2): In; Complete; But Incorrect**

☑ ☑ ☑   **THREE CHECKS (3): In; Complete; Correct**

Figure 2-10
Grading Homework Checklist

HOMEWORK GRADING GUIDE

Question:	Yes	No
1. Can you read the answer?	( )	( )
2. Does it answer the question?	( )	( )
3. Is the answer clear and to the point?	( )	( )
4. Does the answer make sense to you?	( )	( )
5. Could the answer clear up confusion?	( )	( )
6. Do you think the person understands the question?	( )	( )
7. Would this be the answer you would give?	( )	( )
8. Was everything essential included?	( )	( )
9. Would this answer help someone better understand the subject?	( )	( )
10. Did the person do an overall good job?	( )	( )

- -

10 YES = full credit and a "plus"   *3-5 YES = half credit*
6-9 YES = full credit   *0-2 YES = no credit*

Figure 2-11
Homework Grading Guide

Good News About Homework

SCHOOL:_____ DATE:_____

Dear _____,
    I think you should know that _____,
has handed in complete homework for a period of
_____. I have already congratu-
lated _____ on this excellent accomplishment, and I am certain that you will want to add
your personal comments.

_____, Teacher

Figure 2-12
Good News About Homework Note

```
---------------------------------------------------
        I  have  read  the  above  policy  statement
regarding homework for eighth grade students at
Smith Middle School, and I understand its contents.
DATE:_____
PARENT/GUARDIAN SIGNATURE:_____
    (please sign and detach this statement and
     return it to your child's homeroom teacher)
```

Figure 2-13
Home Contact Memo

SPECIAL HOMEWORK NOTICE

Date:_____

Dear _____,

    This is to inform you that _____ currently has ___ undone homework assignments in _____. Since our policy indicates that four undone assignments may equal a reduction in the marking period grade, this is a most serious matter.

    We try to keep the home informed of these matters, for we are certain that you are as concerned as we are about this situation.

    We are sure that you will wish to impress the seriousness of doing homework on your child as we have tried to do here at school.

    We all look forward to more positive contact in the near future.

Teacher:_____

Figure 2-14
Special Homework Notice

Name:_____ Marking Period:_____

Subject:_____

Date of Assignment	Grade Received	Date of Assignment	Grade Received

HW average is found by adding up the grades and dividing by the number of assignments. Remember, 4 "0's" = 1 drop in grade.

Figure 2-15
Homework Grid

RAPID AND EFFICIENT COMMUNICATION

As teachers, what we do most is communicate. We are in constant communication with our students, their parents, the general public, the school's administration and, of course, each other.

Nor is this communication limited to the classroom. It extends to the note from your colleague who needs an answer right now, that call from a student's parent who wanted you to call back as soon as possible, the report on textbook requirements that your department head wanted last Friday, a sample book you wanted to order, the note you must write to Andre's parents regarding his behavior. The list can go on and on.

In this section, let's look at some time-saving techniques that just may lighten that communications load and perhaps even make them more rapid and efficient in the process.

SENDING A LETTER OF INQUIRY

Perhaps you have seen something in a professional magazine that you think might be of interest or use to you in your capacity as a teacher. Perhaps it is an activity that might make an interesting field trip or a packaged art project that your class would enjoy. Whatever it is, you would like to know more about it.

Composing a letter of inquiry can be a time-consuming task, particularly if you must first flesh it out longhand, revise and edit, and finally type it up to send. Even then, isn't there a little buzz at the back of your mind that you may have forgotten to include some needed information?

The form letter in **Figure 3-1** contains appropriate blanks for *all* the information that a letter of inquiry should contain. As such, it certainly helps organize your thoughts so that your inquiry might be precise and exact.

There are two effective ways in which this form can be used. Either you could use it as an example when you compose your own letter, or you could copy the form exactly as you see it and type or write in the required information.

If you do the latter, copy the form onto your school's stationery. Make several copies and keep them at hand in your file cabinet. When the need for a letter of inquiry arises, you have a ready stock that will not only guide you about what must be included, but a form that, once filled out, is ready to mail.

Companies get many, many inquiries each day. According to the sources to whom we've spoken, they do not care whether the letter is formal or informal, handwritten or typed. Their concern is that it is clearly written and contains all the necessary information for a reply.

We think this form will fit the bill for everyone.

REQUESTING A SAMPLE OR SAMPLES

Much of the material we receive through the mail, as well as many of the magazines and periodicals we read as teachers, contain ads for items that we think might play a part in our classrooms. We do not, however, wish to spend cash (our own or the school's) for something that looks good on paper but might be a complete fizzle in practice.

Therefore, we often write to ask for a sample of the product in order to determine if we wish to proceed to order more.

In this regard, we face the same difficulty we did in the previous discussion. Our answer is the same as well.

Figure 3-2 is another form developed specifically for writing for a sample or samples. It is handled in exactly the same way in which you handled the form for the letter of inquiry (see Figure 3-1): Either use it as a guide for your personally written letter, or run it off on your school's stationery and fill in the information that is indicated on the form (either typed or *clearly* handwritten).

Many advertisers will include tear-off cards for free samples, but just as many do not. If you can obtain the sample by checking off a card and dropping it in the mailbox, by all means do so. If something of this type is not included, however, the form in **Figure 3-2** will work well for you. Again, our research has assured us that this contains all the information any company could require in order to send you the sample you are requesting.

This is a time-saver, particularly if you like receiving those free samples and write for many of them.

ORDERING WITHOUT AN ORDER FORM

It has happened to us a number of times. We've spotted something in a magazine or catalog that we really thought would be great for use in our classrooms. The price was right, the item was exactly what we had in mind and *the order form was missing!* Now, what might have been the work of a few minutes stretches out to half an hour or more as we sat down to write a letter ordering the item.

In checking with several companies about this situation, we found that what a supplier really needs for an order is certain information. They need to know your name and address, the address to which to ship the merchandise, a phone number where they can reach you, the item catalog number (if applicable and if known), how many you want, and a description of the item. They would also like you to include state sales tax where applicable and possible shipping and handling charges.

You can include all this information in a letter if you wish, or you can use the form in **Figure 3-3**. This form contains spaces for all the information we have just detailed. This should be copied onto school stationery if you are ordering through the school or onto your own if ordering personally.

As far as tax and handling charges go, if it is a school–related purchase, it may be tax free; so remember to include the school's tax-exempt number. For shipping and handling, you can calculate closely by including $3.00 for the first $10 of your purchase, and add a dollar for every $10 purchased thereafter. If your order comes to $9.95, include $3 handling fee. If it comes to $14.75, include $4; if it is $27.89, the fee would be $5. The maximum sent should be $10 shipping and handling except for unusual items.

If you like to order things through the mail, you will find this form quite helpful for those occasions when the regular order form is nowhere to be found.

WRITING NOTES TO ADMINISTRATION AND COLLEAGUES

We don't know about you, but in the course of our teaching day, we write several notes to either our colleagues or to the administration of the school. Sometimes, these are important notes that need to be handled soon, such as those regarding a student who may have had to be removed from the room. Many times they are requests for anything from having the VCR sent to our room to asking to borrow a felt-tip pen. Others are personal, sometimes even frivolous, and others may simply extend an invitation to share lunch in the Social Studies office. These notes are occasioned by the fact that, once our class has arrived, we are committed to that classroom and cannot leave to attend to other business without someone qualified taking our place.

So the note becomes an efficient means of communication throughout the school.

A group of teachers developed the all-purpose form that may be seen in **Figure 3-4**. This was reduced, placed four on a page, and run off on the copier in quantity. A student aide with a paper cutter made the whole into its parts, and these were distributed to the teachers who thought it up.

Thereafter, it became an easy matter to send notes. No longer did you have to search for paper and take the time to compose a message. *In the majority of cases*, a check and a word or two was sufficient to communicate the message. It became a very quick and, for them, a very efficient manner of sending notes to the administration and to each other during the school day.

Most certainly, if you are going to use something like this, you should adapt it to your school, your colleagues, and your administration. If some of the messages seem a bit too "breezy" for you or your school, then by all means change them to meet your needs. This example suited one group of teachers under their particular set of circumstances. If *you* use it, make it your own.

While you might certainly have occasion to write longer and more involved notes as the situation warrants, something like this saves you a good amount of time and trouble for the majority of your daily note-writing tasks.

WRITING NOTES TO PARENTS

Can a teacher get through a school year without writing a note to at least one parent? Impossible! Whether you write formal progress reports half-way through a marking period as required by your school or department, or issue warning notices for students experiencing academic difficulties, or make a written attempt to contact the home about missing homework, you *will* be writing notes to parents as a part of your teaching day.

While no one can tell you what to write, since no one knows your situation but you, we can share something with you about writing notes to parents that has proven helpful for others in achieving a positive home-school rapport, while saving a great deal of time for the teachers involved!

Look at **Figure 3-5**. During the first week or two of the school year, all students in the class receive these with their names written in the appropriate place. They are to bring them home for their parents.

As you can see, the goal of this note is to establish rapport with the home and gently indicate that it is not possible for you to handwrite 125 letters to the parents and guardians of all the children in your classes. It is brief and to the point. Thereafter, when you must communicate with the home through forms, such as a check-off Progress Report, you will have already established the fact in their minds that this is not impersonal, just expedient.

But—and here is the biggest bonus you will get out of this—if you should have to personally contact the home of a specific student via a personal letter or even a lengthy telephone conversation, the basis for understanding and cooperation will have already been implanted. We have already spoken about the use of positive home contact in regard to homework (Figures 2-12–2-14) and the benefits that it can bring you. Here is another method of establishing a rapport with the home so that, when you really must contact the home for a serious reason, there is receptiveness to your suggestions and input.

Certainly, this seems a simple technique, but you really should give it a try. Other notes of this type given throughout the year (the holidays, just before mid-winter break or spring break, and other times) continue to cement the home-school relationship that will serve you well when you need it.

For the relatively small amount of time invested, it reaps large dividends.

ANSWERING THE PARENTAL NOTE

Let's assume that you have established home-school rapport as indicated in the previous discussion. Perhaps you have even continued this rapport by contacting the home about homework (Figures 2-12–2-14). So far, the discussion has been about your sending notes to parents. Let's examine what happens when it is the other way around.

Most notes from parents (or so we have found) are easily handled. In this regard, one of the greatest time-savers when dealing with the easy note is to answer it the moment you get it. Suppose Lou Ann gives you a note from her mom at the beginning of class. The moment the class has been assigned some work that allows you to direct your attention to it, answer the note. You'll be surprised how short a time it takes if you do it immediately. Moreover, Lou Ann has it by the end of class to take home.

That's for the easy note. Suppose, however, you receive a note (such as the one received by a teacher we know) in which the parent threatened legal action were a grade not changed immediately. This is *not* one to answer on the spur of the moment. You need time to think, to organize and perhaps to seek advice. The note need not be as threatening as in the example, but a request for assignments and material to be covered for the next two weeks is not something to be tossed off in a minute, either. In both cases, you need time.

The form reply seen in **Figure 3-6** will buy you that time. This *is* something that can be filled out immediately and sent home with the student at once. It acknowledges the communication from home, indicates that a reply *is* forthcoming and sets a date in the future when your reply will be forthcoming. This allows you to give yourself the time you need to cool down, seek advice, get the information you need, copy the documents required and so on. Make the reply time-reasonable (two days hence is suggested), and you will be able to prepare the precise reply that is needed, free from immediate stress and with informed knowledge.

In the long run, that will save not only time but a great deal of frustration as well.

SENDING GOOD OR PLEASANT NEWS

We know that we have been stressing the benefits of establishing positive home-school relations as a basis for working with problems should they arise later. We do this because we have been witness to how this expedient works so well. Let us tell you about a case in point.

One day, the faculty of a middle school arrived to find huge piles of the form seen in **Figure 3-7**, along with a sign that advised teachers to take as many as they wished. At a faculty meeting scheduled for that afternoon, the principal, who had supplied the forms, asked the faculty to try them out, to use them to communicate some good or pleasant news when a child had done something that would warrant such a positive note.

What is there to explain about this form? If a child got an A+ on a test, a simple message ("Dolly got an A+ on the test! Great!") would do just fine. "Scott was a great help to me today" is another message that comes to mind. You get the idea. This form is for *good* news.

Several teachers began to use this, and soon most of the faculty was using it as well. The reason: It works. After a relatively short time, home-school rapport was blossoming. No records were kept on results, but the perception of the teachers who used this was that cooperation from the home decidedly increased, with a subsequent rise in the performance of the students.

Ask the teachers involved, and they will tell you that it was well worth the small amount of effort it took to write out a short line.

If you try this, you'll like it, and you'll enjoy the positive results as well.

COMMUNICATING BAD OR UNPLEASANT NEWS

The previous technique works wonderfully in establishing rapport by sending home good news from school. As we all know, however, not all the news the home receives from school is of a positive nature. Throughout a school year, the teacher is bound to have to contact the home about poor behavior, assignments not done, bad grades, an incident with another child and so on. When this happens, it is time for another approach.

It is a matter of personal philosophy, of course, but we always handwrite notes to home about problems. It seems more personal. While no parent enjoys getting bad news from school, the news can be made a bit more palatable if the note is conscientiously crafted.

Figure 3-8 is an example of such a note. It reflects what is required in a letter of this type.

First, it identifies with the home. It is neither solely the home's problem nor the teacher's; it is "our" problem. It is identified as such.

Next, it offers hope for the future and places the problem in perspective. If the home is overwhelmed by the greatness of the problem, you could well see no action at all. This approach lets the home see the incident within the entire scheme of school and assures them that this, too, will pass.

Third, the problem is stated clearly. It is made simple to understand. Also, what you, as the teacher, want done is clearly stated. There can be no misperception as to the incident or the course of action you wish to pursue.

Finally, the help of the home is enlisted, not demanded. A demand that the home take a specific action can easily get you no action at all. Note again that the teacher identifies with the home and offers hope for an amicable solution.

While this is no positive guarantee that the home will cooperate, we feel that this stands a much better chance of enlisting cooperation than does a more blunt and matter-of-fact note that does not take these factors into consideration.

Does this save time? Well, if it works (which it does more often than not), your problem with the student is on its way to being solved. That alone is certainly worth the effort.

RETURNING AND MAKING PHONE CALLS

Aren't you glad the telephone was invented? How could we get through our teaching day without using the telephone at least once: taking a message and returning a call to someone who wanted us to get back within the next 30 seconds? If all this sounds facetious, that's because it is. Nonetheless, dealing with our daily telephone messages and the calls we must make can be a tiresome and time-consuming task.

What complicates the process is the fact that, as teachers, we live by a schedule. If our next class begins at 10:45, we must be at that classroom at precisely

10:45. We cannot say, "Well, I'll just make one more call. The class will wait for me. We'll start at 11:00 today." You know how impossible that is. Whatever you may be doing on the phone, that conversation must end in time for you to meet your obligation to your next class.

Let us share with you two ideas that have helped teachers successfully manage their telephone time.

The first method is something really simple that works wonders. Establish and let it be known far and wide that there is one time during the day *and one time only* when you will make and return phone calls—and stick to it!

Do you have a professional, nonteaching or preparation period in your schedule? Is that when you will have time for phone calls? Then inform everyone—your students, their parents, the main office, the administration—that this and this alone is the time you are available for making and returning calls. There may be some hitches at first, but if you stick to that schedule, it will soon become known to all, and that is the only time you will have to bother with the telephone. It will become automatic for the school secretary to take a call for you and tell the caller, "Mrs. Smith will get back to you between 1:10 and 1:45 this afternoon" or "Mr. Jones makes all calls between 11:00 and 11:30; I'll inform him of your call."

Another time-saver for telephone conversations is to have a script before you for each call you make. **Figure 3-9** is an example of a short script that you would fill in with the main points you wished to cover during your call. They might be the items with catalog numbers and descriptions that you wish to order from the company you are calling, or they might be three points you wish to make about that young man who threw the geraniums across the room this morning. As each point is covered, you can check off the space provided, thereby indicating that you have communicated that fact. In this manner, you will be able to see where you are going, see where you have been and keep the conversation from straying to unrelated topics. At the end of the conversation, you also have a dated record of what was said and when it was communicated.

Although both these methods are fairly simple to implement, they will save you a great deal of time and frustration in dealing with those school-related telephone calls.

STRATEGIES FOR THE COMMUNICATION OF DISPLEASURE

We have made the point several times before that, when things are going well, you should communicate that pleasure to others in order to build a positive rapport. However, some of the things that happen in school and in our classrooms do not cause us joy. On the contrary, many incidents, particularly those involving our students, cause us displeasure. When that happens, how do we communicate that fact?

We all realize that a wrong word, spoken in anger, extreme stress or frustration, can often cause a setback in everything we have been trying to do; it can place roadblocks in the way of positive cooperation and take us back to start.

Here are three strategies for handling the communication of your displeasure (whatever the cause) that work well in all situations.

First, wherever possible, don't react immediately. Put some distance between the incident and yourself. We knew a teacher who refused to discipline on the day an incident happened. He maintained that if he did, he would be doing something to punish the child. On the other hand, if he waited until the heat of the moment had passed, his discipline would be aimed at bringing the child back to correct behavior. That is no small distinction! It will save you time and a great deal of trouble if you wait until the situation and you have cooled down.

Next, write down what happened and what you want to happen. Do this after the "cooling-down" period. Relate the incident in calm and rational language. Of course, avoid phrases like "in a cowardly and sneaky fashion" or "with eyes glowing hatred." Stick to the facts. Also, write down what you want to have happen. Do you want Allan to (1) apologize to Miranda for hitting her with a spitball, (2) be given some sort of punishment for his spitball act, or (3) stop shooting spitballs in the future? Then write out these objectives in exactly that order. The self-explanatory form in **Figure 3-10** guides you in doing what we have just been talking about, and provides a written record of both the incident and your reaction to it.

Finally—and this is very important—have someone you trust look over or appraise your response before you make it. One of the hallmarks of our profession is the fact that we help each other and share techniques in order to grow, both for ourselves and our students. Use that professionalism now. Before you communicate your displeasure, share what you are going to say or write with a colleague, and make certain it is someone who likes you enough to tell you that you are wrong if he or she feels that way. If so, consider rephrasing or rewriting.

Is this a time-saver? If you consider the consequences—both to you as a teacher and to your class—of hasty, heated and improper communication of your displeasure, then believe us, this is well worth every second it takes.

INSTANT REFERRAL OF STUDENT FOR DISCIPLINARY REASONS

While the vast majority of cases involving inappropriate or disrupting behavior can be and are handled within the confines of the classroom by the teacher alone, there will inevitably be the incident in which the student involved must be removed from the room. Indeed, whether formally as part of policy or informally as part of a general understanding within the school, certain behaviors almost automatically call for removal. We know of one school, for instance, where any physical violence—hitting, slapping or throwing an object at another student—is to be immediately reported to the main office and the child is to be instantly removed from the situation. This is part of that school's policy.

Along with every removal, there is inevitably a process to be followed. We know of no school where this does not involve the writing up of the student. Whether they are called "Discipline Slips" or "Student Referral Forms," most schools have some sort of paper that must be filled out when a student is removed from the room.

All this is fine on paper. But what happens when the flames of the situation are burning all about us, when the tenseness of the moment threatens to send the class into panic, when the incident is headed for dangerous grounds and lack of control? Then what you want and need to do is to get the kid out of the room as quickly as possible. You should *not* take the time to fill out the referral form while the child further disrupts the class, nor can you put the child in the hallway while you do it, since that is only an invitation to disaster.

Here's something that has worked well in handling this tense situation. Make several copies of the card seen in **Figure 3-11**. Keep them handy in your desk. If an incident requiring student removal occurs, forget about the standard referral sheet. Take one of these, write down the student's name and the date, give it to him or her and get the kid out of the room. Using this card, the entire process should take less than 15 seconds.

If you have an intercom system in your school, it would be well to take a few more seconds to inform the main office that the child has been removed from your room and should be on the way to the main office even as you speak.

Having removed the student instantly, you can now concentrate on getting back to instruction following the disruptive incident as we discussed in Section One for Figure 1-14 (Emergency Interruption List). Later in the day, when the stress on you and the situation has subsided, you will be in a much better position to fill out referral forms required by your school.

This expedient has proven to be not only a time-saver but a trouble-saver as well.

COMPLETING REPORTS FOR ADMINISTRATION

Writing reports seems to be as much a part of teaching as writing on the chalkboard or writing a comment on a student's paper. Indeed, some days seem to be taken up with furnishing reports of every conceivable nature to Guidance, the Child Study Team, and the school administration. Of course, these reports are necessary and meaningful for the functioning of the modern school, and naturally it is part and parcel of our job to supply them as required. Even so, it is often a time-consuming and tiresome process.

Let us share with you some ideas for expeditiously handling the many reports that come our way during the school year.

First, consider keeping a Teacher Report File. This could be a regular file folder kept in your file cabinet or a notebook or report folder kept in your desk. In it place all the forms and papers that you will require for the reports that you must submit. Get several copies of each and keep them handy. Then, when it is time to prepare a report, you don't have to go looking for the proper form or make one or two unnecessary trips to various offices to pick them up. You will have saved some time before you even begin.

Next, devote a section of your planbook or marking book to that material and information you will need for those reports. You understand that we cannot tell you what to keep in that section—that will have to be determined by the nature of the reports required of you. Perhaps it will be running totals of class or homeroom attendance, perhaps a list of children who returned or did not return certain insurance forms, perhaps an indication of absences or homework not handed in or children whose parents want to join the PTA—whatever is required of you in reports that *your* school must have.

The reason is obvious. How much time will you save if the information you need for the report is right at your fingertips? A great deal, of course, and it will be considerably less frustrating as well.

Finally, keep a running record of serious problems that need to be reported. In "Dealing with the Serious and Prolonged Behavioral Problem" (page 13), we detailed an extremely efficient method for doing this, and you might like to look that over again. The value of such a record is that, when it comes time to report on a serious problem such as a student with extreme behavioral difficulties, you will have all the information you need, as well as a written record of the problem and your attempts to handle it. At the end of Section One, we suggested keeping a memo pad on each separate problem, but it might be just as effective if you dedicated a separate section of your planbook or markbook to this process.

It has never thrilled us with joy to have to make out a required report, even though we realize their value. These methods will help the reports get done a little quicker and a great deal more smoothly.

That's no small accomplishment.

PREPARING AND PUBLISHING AN ITINERARY

One of the tasks that we have always found arduous is the preparing of an itinerary for class field trips. Certainly, these are necessary. They inform the school where you will be in the event that an emergency should occur. They inform the faculty of your whereabouts and the whereabouts of students who may be going. And they even serve as a reminder to you of what is next on the agenda and a general time frame in which to operate. Even so, it can be quite a task drawing one up.

A two-step process, however, will make it a little easier.

First, keep all the information about the trip in a central place. Start a file folder the moment the trip is suggested, and in it keep all brochures, schedules, contracts and other materials that deal with that trip. You now have *one* place to go to get any information you will need in planning and drawing up your itinerary.

Then use the form in **Figure 3-12** to help you prepare the document. As you look it over, we hope you will see that it contains spaces for all appropriate information that the school could require of you for an itinerary of the day's trip. All you do is copy it and fill it in. If you've kept all the pertinent information in one place, that should be fairly easy. If you need more space for the names of the children going, you need only add another plain typed sheet.

Typical entries on this sheet might be as follows:

8:30   Leave school via two buses (Smith Transport)
9:15   Arrive at Newtown Aquarium, 165 Rt.#100 (555-5555)
9:30   Dolphin Show at Aquarium

And so it would go, with your final entry being, "Arrive back at school."

One final hint: At the beginning of the school term, type up a list of all the children in your classes. Then, when you have to publish a list of those going somewhere, copy the list, black or white out the names of those not going, and copy the list again. That's an incredibly quick way to prepare a list of those going.

You're going to save lots of time and trouble using this method.

DEALING WITH EMERGENCY COMMUNICATIONS

A detailed itinerary like that in the last discussion becomes essential when handling an emergency such as a tragedy in a child's family. With this document available, the boy or girl can be quickly found.

Indeed, it need not be a catastrophic incident to fall into the emergency communication category. We don't have to detail for you several situations in which you might want the building principal or vice-principal *"on the double,"* situations in which the child's home needs to be notified *by the end of the school day*, situations in which you need something or someone, and *now!* In an emergency communication, time is of the essence, and you cannot afford to wait.

Let us give you a method we have used to handle these situations, and then let us add a most important caution.

This may sound simple, but hear it through. People react swiftly and certainly to come to your aid in an emergency *if they are certain that it is an emergency.* Consider these words:

Please help.

Now look at the same words a little differently:

Please! HELP!!!

Which would you respond to quicker? The first seems like a polite request, with no urgency. The second tells of a "right now" need.

Look at **Figure 3-13**. We did several of these on regular 3×5-inch index cards, which we kept in the desk. Within the first month of class, a boy had a very bad seizure, in a room that had no intercom. The card was pulled out, "Nurse—205" was scrawled across it, and a child was dispatched to the main office. In an amazingly short time, not only the nurse, but the principal, vice-principal, and

Head Guidance Counselor appeared at the door, and the child got the help he needed.

If you are sending this home, the message may be considerably longer, but the point is that your emergency communication gets noticed and gets read.

Caution: This is an extremely effective technique, *provided that you do not use it too often*. Save this for true emergencies only, and it will get fast and complete results. Use this every time you want the guidance counselor to speak to Barry about his homework, and, like the boy and the wolf, soon no one will take notice and the entire process will have lost its effectiveness.

Used properly, this gets results—quickly!

HANDLING THOSE COMMON REQUESTS

It would be naive and certainly misleading to suppose that all communications in teaching are emergencies. Certainly, if we take the total number of communications handled by a teacher during any given school year, those of an emergency nature would comprise a small percentage of them. Most of our communications would revolve around relatively simple, common requests.

A colleague writes a note asking if he might borrow a red pen; the secretary wonders when she will receive those PTA forms from your homeroom; the guidance counselor wants to know if you have gotten back all those schedule requests.

These are simple requests, but when you have enough of them, you can find yourself sacrificing class time to keep up with the demands. Let's discuss some ways in which we can handle those common requests with efficiency and dispatch.

First, if it is at all possible, handle the request the moment it comes in. Requests that pile up, even simple ones, can create a logjam in your day. If a child delivers a note, and you can answer that note by sending something back with the child, or by writing a few words on the note that was sent to you and sending it back with the deliverer, then by all means do so. Get it over with, and it will no longer be there to take your time.

Toward this end, you might recall Figure 3-4 earlier in this section. This is a place where it could be effectively used as the need dictated.

If the request is of such a nature that it cannot be answered immediately, however, it will save you a great deal of misunderstanding if you will acknowledge the request and set a time for answering it. **Figure 3-14** is an example of something that fills the bill and may be placed on a memo pad sheet or a standard index card. It acknowledges the receipt of the note, so that the sender knows that you are working on the request, and it sets a definite time when you will have the answer. This is very useful when your answer requires that you do some research or get some documents together that will take a little time. It has forestalled many a misunderstanding.

Certainly, for a longer and more involved request or in answering a letter from the home, your response is going to be more detailed and more formal. The procedures in this section, however, work fine in handling those common requests and communications we face each day.

Date:_____

To: _____
_____
_____
_____

Greetings:

I am seeking some information, and I believe that you can help me. I wish to inquire about the following:

_____
_____
_____

This came to my attention via the following:

_____
_____

What I need to know is:

_____
_____
_____

Please send this information to:

_____
_____
_____
_____

Here is some other information you may need to know:
My Position:_____ Daytime Tel. No.:_____
Institution:_____

Thank you for your kind and prompt attention to this matter.

Yours sincerely,

_____
Title:_____

Figure 3-1
Informational Inquiry Letter Form

Date: _____

To: _____

_____

_____

_____

Greetings:

I would like to receive from you the following sample(s):

_____

_____

_____

I became aware of this from the following source:

_____

_____

Please send the sample(s) to the following address:

_____

_____

_____

Here is additional information you may care to know:

My Position: _____   Daytime Tel. No.: _____

School: _____

Samples to be evaluated for: _____

_____

Additional Comments: _____

_____

_____

Thank you for your prompt attention to this request.

Yours sincerely,

_____

Title: _____

Figure 3-2
Request for Samples Form

Date: _____

To: _____

_____

_____

_____

Greetings:

I would like to order the item(s) listed below. I became aware of this merchandise in the following manner:

_____

_____

This is the merchandise I wish to purchase:

Cat. #	Quant.	Item and Description	Price	Total

Please ship the order to:

_____

_____

_____

Here is some additional information you may require:

Order for: ( ) individual ( ) school Tax Exempt No.:_____

Purchase Sub-Total: $_____ Sales Tax: _____

Shipping & Handling: _____ Order Total: _____

Person Ordering: _____ Title: _____

Institution:_____

Daytime Tel. No. _____ Special Instructions: _____

_____

Thank you for your prompt attention to this order.

Yours sincerely,

_____

Title: _____

Figure 3-3
All-Purpose Order Form

To:_____ Date:_____

From:_____

[ ]   **May I borrow** _____

[ ]   **Do you have**_____

[ ]   **Can we meet? When:**_____ **Where:**_____

[ ]   **Meeting on** _____ **at** _____ **in**

_____**regarding**_____

[ ]   **Please send me this student:**_____

       [ ] Now   **[ ] End of Class**

[ ]   **Do you know the location of**_____

[ ]   **Student** _____**is late to your class.**

I kept this student.   Time sent: _____

[ ]   **Please read the attached and get back to me.**

[ ]   **The attached is "For Your Eyes Only."**

[ ]   **I'd like to discuss the following:** _____

_____

[ ]   **May I have your wisdom on** _____

_____

_____

[ ]   **Special message:** _____

_____

_____

[ ]   **Reply:** _____

_____

_____

_____

Figure 3-4
Quick Note to Colleagues Checklist

Dear _____,

     I am truly sorry that time does not permit me to write a personal note to the parents of every student in the class, but I am certain that you understand how much there is to do for the education of your child and how short time can be.

     I am _____'s teacher, and I look forward to meeting you at the various parent functions that will be held throughout the school year. When we meet face to face, we will have a chance to get better acquainted, I am certain.

     From time to time throughout this coming year, I will be sending home various letters, forms and other documents. If you receive a form letter from me, it is not meant to be impersonal, merely to save time and devote attention to my students. I thank you in advance for understanding.

     I am looking forward to a great year and to meeting you soon.

                 Yours sincerely,

                 _____, *Teacher*

Figure 3-5
Rapport With Parents Note

Date:_____

Dear _____,

     I am in receipt of your message dated _____.
Thank you for writing.

     I will reply on _____,
as my schedule permits.

     Thank you for being understanding.

                 _____, **Teacher**

Figure 3-6
Receipt of Parental Note Form

| SMITH MIDDLE SCHOOL | The "Good News" TELEGRAM | SMITH MIDDLE SCHOOL |

Here is some GOOD NEWS from school:

_____

_____

_____

_____

_____

_____

_____

_____

_____

_____

_____

Figure 3-7
The "Good News" Telegram

Dear _____,

A problem has arisen regarding _____'s performance in school. It is something which we can handle together, and when the home and school cooperate as we shall be doing, _____ will be soon back to his/her usual level of accomplishment.

You see, _____ hasn't been handing in his/her homework assignments. He/She is currently missing ____ of them, and one more assignment not completed could have an effect upon his/her marking period grade. _____ is too good a student to allow that to happen, and that is what has occasioned this note to you.

_____ will have homework every night next week. I will be checking it in school, and I'm hoping that you will supervise its completion at home. With all of us pitching in, I'm certain that _____ will soon be back to his/her usual productivity.

I like _____, and I know that through our joint effort, this "glitch" in his/her academic life will soon pass.

I'll keep you informed. Call me if you like.

Sincerely,

_____, Teacher

Figure 3-8
Reporting Bad News (Sample letter)

TELEPHONE CONVERSATION ITINERARY

Caller:_____ Date:_____

Person called:_____

Telephone number called:_____

Subject of call:_____

_____

Points to cover   **Covered**

_____
_____   [ ]
_____
_____   [ ]
_____
_____   [ ]
_____
_____   [ ]
_____
_____   [ ]
_____
_____   [ ]
_____
_____   [ ]

Notes

_____
_____
_____
_____
_____
_____
_____
_____
_____

Figure 3-9
Telephone Conversation Itinerary

CLASSROOM INCIDENT REPORT

Teacher:_____ **Date:**_____

Student(s) Involved in Incident:

_____

_____

Describe What Happened (facts only, please):

_____

_____

_____

_____

_____

_____

What Would You Like to See Happen Now:

_____

_____

_____

_____

_____

_____

Signature of Teacher:_____

Figure 3-10
Classroom Incident Report

Date:_____

It has become necessary to remove

Student:_____

from my class. Please handle this now, and I will supply all necessary forms as soon as possible.

Teacher:_____
Room :_____

Figure 3-11
Instant Disciplinary Referral Card

CLASS TRIP INFORMATION

Teacher in Charge:_____ Date of Trip:_____
Destination:_____
Telephone Number(s) at Destination:_____
Time Frame: Leave School:_____ Return to School:_____
Teachers/Chaperones Going:_____
_____
_____

TRIP ITINERARY

Time	Location/Destination/Activity (include telephone # where possible)

STUDENTS GOING ON TRIP

attach additional sheets as needed

Figure 3-12
Trip Itinerary Preparation Form

! IMMEDIATE ATTENTION !

Teacher: _____

Figure 3-13
Immediate Attention Card

Date:_____

I have received your message re:

_____

I will get back to you about this on or before:

_____

_____,Teacher

Figure 3-14
Get-Back-to-You-Soon Card

SECTION

4

ENHANCING YOUR RECORDKEEPING EFFICIENCY

If we were to informally poll the teachers we know and ask them to list their least favorite teaching-related chore, we are willing to venture that the most frequent response would be *recordkeeping*. While we certainly appreciate that no school system can function without the accurate keeping of records, that admission does little to help us get through the hours we spend on the task.

In this section, we'll look at several techniques that have worked in reducing the time spent keeping those records, while handling them efficiently and effectively. From records on the first day of school to making certain that all records are complete and up to date, let's examine some ways of easing the recordkeeping burden.

HANDLING THE FIRST-DAY-OF-SCHOOL INFORMATION

In our school, there has never been an opening day when homeroom has not been extended well into first and even second period. There is just too much to do on that first meeting of the first day of the new school year. Insurance forms, PTA information, locker keys or combinations, attendance data, emergency information forms, and more have to be filled out, collected, alphabetized and the like. We know of many teachers who find this opening day onslaught of recordkeeping to be not only time-consuming but frustrating as well.

Here's another case where spending a little time will save you a great deal of time and energy. Begin by determining what has to be done and what forms need to be distributed. Take these forms and place one of each on every desk in the classroom that is to be occupied. When you are finished, you will have a packet of forms, cards, brochures, handbooks, and so on, on each desk. Now take some 3×5 inch index cards and write one of your student's names on each card. If so inclined or if there is no objection from your school, you might even write the child's locker number and/or combination on the card. Finally, place that card on top of the pile of forms on the desk you wish that student to occupy. This is done the day before the opening day or that morning before the children arrive.

When the first day of school comes, as the children file into the room (ours arrive in staggered fashion due to a high percentage of students coming by bus), they are told to find their names and sit in those seats. When the bell rings for class, you now have the class in their assigned seats according to your seating chart, with all materials already in front of them, ready to begin. There is no confusion, nor is time wasted handing out forms and making sure that everyone has the same documents. They are all there and ready.

If a child doesn't show up, you collect the materials from his or her desk and place them in a manila envelope with the child's name on it. Not only does that help with attendance, but all forms are ready and waiting should that student come in the next day.

If desired, you might want to make up and include a form such as that in **Figure 4-1**. This simple check-off list will remind students of what they must do, have done, or need to do. The part at the bottom will also act as a deterrent from the protest that they never received a particular form or didn't understand it.

The first day is still going to be hectic, but good organization helps it flow smoothly.

OBTAINING STUDENT PERSONAL DATA

Of course, the school keeps records on each student. These records include a great deal of useful information such as a student's address, telephone number, name of parent and guardian if different, and so forth. Indeed, this is often essential information when it comes time to contact the home about the student.

One problem we have found is that, while this information is available to teachers, it is often inconvenient to use, because it is in the school vault (so to speak) while you are in your classroom, half a school-length away, when you need it.

Toward solving that problem, we have each child in each class fill out a regular index card with all the information we feel we will need over the coming year. A problem we encountered was that the information supplied by the students was not always accurate, and often there were things we should have known that the child never put down or considered important.

We still have the kids fill out the index card to be filed in our records, but now we send home that card along with the note in **Figure 4-2**. That note is rather self-explanatory, and when the index card comes back to you, you now have accurate information along with any special insights you, as a teacher, might need to know to make your dealings with students and their families run smoothly.

This simple procedure has proven beneficial for our functioning throughout the school year.

EFFECTIVELY KEEPING TEXTBOOK RECORDS

Textbooks are given out for a student's use over a school year. They are expected to be returned at the end of that year with only one year of wear evident. It does not always work out that way.

Students sometimes lose books, rip pages, abuse books, lend them to other students and forget who has them. When this happens it is essential that the teacher has kept good textbook records in order that the confusion may be set straight.

Let's look at two techniques for enhancing the keeping of textbook records.

The first suggestion comes from a teacher who advises us to keep that textbook record in our marking book. After she has listed the names of the class in her marking book, this teacher draws a two-inch column directly beside their names.

In this space, she records the book number (writing one on the inside cover of each book if it does not have one already) and the general condition of the book issued.

Now, at any time during the year, should a problem with a book arise, she has all the information at her fingertips without having to retrieve it from a distant file cabinet. Moreover, the recording of condition precludes disagreements about the abuse of the book that may occur when it comes back. It has saved her a good deal of time and argument.

This second suggestion deals with problems of lost books, switched books or books that were lent and never returned. One teacher records a small number on a page within the body of each text. The number is different for each book. If you picked up one of his texts you might find a small "25" written in ink in the lower left-hand corner of page 147. When recording textbook distribution, he also records the secret number for each book. Later, if a dispute arises as to the possession of a text, he need only check his hidden mark to settle the situation. This has proven beneficial to him, particularly when the book in question had the name of the original student blotted out and another written in its stead.

He claims that in all the years he has been using this technique, not one student has ever realized that the small number on page 147 was his secret code.

We have used both of these procedures, and they really are recordkeeping helps.

HANDLING CLASS ATTENDANCE RECORDS

Most of us make an effort to take daily class attendance, realizing that it may be required in a number of instances. Perhaps the main office is inquiring about a child's attendance on a particular day last month, or perhaps it may be required as proof in order to implement a school policy on the number of absences prior to withholding of credit. Attendance is necessary. And just the day that you are running short on time and forget to take it will be the day that Guidance or the Main Office wants to know about!

We'd solve that problem by allowing a student aide to take your daily classroom attendance. This task can be made simple, quick and efficient for the aide through the use of the form in **Figure 4-3**.

Do not leave this in the student aide's possession. Keep it in your classroom or in the back of your marking book, and give it to the aide each day or have the aide take it, as you desire. If the names of the students are listed down the side, it is an easy task to fill in the blank under a particular day with the proper attendance code. We can recommend the code at the bottom of **Figure 4-3**, or use any one that suits you.

Once a particular month has ended, this form can be kept in your file cabinet, ready for reference should you need it. Even were you not present to explain it, it would be easily decipherable and anyone could find the particular month, day, class and period required.

Another advantage is that you don't have to use up whole sections of your marking book for attendance or keep a separate attendance book.

Once in practice, it becomes a regular part of each day's classroom routine and no longer interferes with your teaching time.

HANDLING SCHOOL ATTENDANCE RECORDS

The previous discussion dealt with the handling of attendance within each individual class. Now let's talk about the attendance that you take for the benefit of the entire school.

Most schools have already established a procedure for the recording of daily attendance. These procedures vary slightly from school to school. But most of them still revolve around a central theme—you, the teacher, taking attendance in a particular class and reporting it to a central location.

So many variables are involved that it is difficult to think of any expedient other than checking each seat and listing those not present (or pulling their cards or typing in a number or however your school may handle it). Under certain circumstances, however, there are some techniques that help.

Try taking a class list and posting one each day, perhaps on a clipboard hung from the wall near the entrance to the classroom. As students come into homeroom (or wherever else your school takes daily attendance), they place their initials beside their names. When the bell rings, you remove the clipboard and your attendance is already taken.

For lower grades, you might want to try the poster in **Figure 4-4**. In one pocket are cards or slips with the children's names. As a child comes into class, he or she takes the slip with the proper name and transfers it to the other pocket. At the proper time, the teacher or student aide who is handling attendance records the names on the cards still left in the first pocket.

Caution: If you should try either of these, you must remember that until this is a *well-established* part of daily routine, children will forget to sign in or move a card. It is also possible that some prankster will sign in for or move the card of someone not present. In short, it will need supervision until it is taken seriously by the class.

RECORDING QUIZ AND TEST SCORES

What goes into making up a marking period grade? There are as many answers to that as there are teachers, but part of the answer must certainly be an average of the tests and quizzes taken by a student over the marking period.

If your marking book is like ours, it is filled with information. Homework done and undone, special marks for special projects, perhaps attendance, perhaps a daily class performance—all are there along with the scores from quizzes and tests.

It will make your life easier and your averaging a great deal more expeditious if you keep those quiz grades *together* in one place and those test results *together* in another separate place.

Figure 4-5 offers a form that you make up and copy, assigning one for each of your classes for a given marking period. Since the form is really self-explanatory, we will simply say that there is space for the date and content of each test or quiz, they are grouped together in separate places and the setup, we feel, makes it easy to calculate a test average and a quiz average. Moreover, at the end of each marking period, you have a very nice and easily handled record of the hard grades that went into determining a student's full marking period score.

When you no longer have to go searching for something, when it is all together for you in one convenient spot, when the very proximity of the grades makes averaging easier, then this is an excellent way to save time and make your academic life a little easier.

USING STUDENT AIDES FOR RECORDKEEPING

So far in this section, we have done a lot of talking about using student aides to help in your daily recordkeeping tasks. It would be well, therefore, if we spoke for a moment about handling those student aides who can save you so much time.

It will save you trouble if you follow a few standard guidelines for properly using student aides. An irresponsible or unconcerned student can make repeated mistakes in the tasks assigned, and that can lead to all sorts of difficulties.

First, select an alternate or backup for each aide you select. This is particularly important in such tasks as taking attendance, since this is a daily process, and you want someone there if the assigned student is absent of a day. Both the aide and his or her alternate should be fully trained in what you desire of them. Even if the aide in question has a perfect attendance record, every so often allow the alternate to do the process for a day. This keeps the alternate ready to step in should the regular student aide be missing.

Next, evaluate the performance of student aides and change them if need be. You can't fire a student aide, because they are not employed. If, however, after repeated warnings and repeated instances of an improperly done or incomplete task, there has been no improvement, then perhaps that student should be assigned another area in which to help out. Never assume that student aides will simply continue to perform perfectly for the rest of the year. Such an assumption could be deadly for you and your recordkeeping. Evaluate their performance and replace them as necessary.

Finally, select your student aides on the basis of what you are trying to accomplish. If what you want to do is to save yourself time and effort (which is perfectly legitimate), then from your volunteers, you might want to select those you feel most capable of performing at a high level. Also remember that functioning as a student aide can be a learning experience, developing responsibility and pride of performance in the student involved. One teacher we know arranges it so that *every student in his class* gets to function as a student aide at some time during the marking period. If you feel this way, you should realize that not every student will perform equally well, and closer supervision of students with special needs will be required.

It all depends on what you want to get out of it. Done properly, according to the goals you set and with an eye toward the evaluation of their performance, using student aides can prove to be a very positive experience, both for you and for your students.

TAKING A COUNT FOR CLASS OR SCHOOL RECORDS

"The Yearbook Committee would like to know how many of you would be interested in purchasing a yearbook if the price were between $20 and $30? While we're at it, how many of you would be interested in going on a Saturday trip for supervised skiing? And, by the way, our own field trip is coming up soon, so how many are definitely not going on that trip?"

Does that sound familiar? Very often, teachers are asked to take a number of counts for recordkeeping purposes. If it is something relatively short, perhaps a show of hands will do, but what if there are a number of questions or what if answering in public might embarrass a child (if a child, for instance, does not have the money to go on a trip)? And what if, after the count is taken and reported, a student claims that he or she said yes instead of no and demands to be included even though there are no more seats available?

For taking any kind of count that applies to a recordkeeping nature, we'd suggest using the form in **Figure 4-6**. You make up (or copy) this form and write down the names of the students in your class *once*, then run off as many copies as you need to make a good sized stack of them. When a question arises that requires a count, you fill in the information at the top and hand the form to the first student in a row. Thereafter, you go about your teaching as the sheet circulates among the students. There is minimal interruption of teaching time.

When you get the sheet back, you can easily tally the count in a few seconds. Virtually no time has been lost.

Furthermore, after you have sent in your count, be certain to retain this form. Since each student is asked to confirm his or her choice with initials, you have not only a record of how each student reacted to the question, but you also have incontrovertible evidence of what a student elected, should a disagreement occur.

Of course, you are always going to get the occasional youngster who will not take this form seriously, but that is easily handled if you remain consistent in your discipline, and the benefits are really positive. You will like using this.

TAKING A LUNCH COUNT

In many schools, particularly those without a large cafeteria, teachers are required to take a count of the students who will be buying lunch on a particular day. This lunch count must be delivered to some authority by a certain time each day so that an estimated number of student lunches can be prepared. The same process might apply to taking a count for milk, cookies, snacks and more. Let us share with you how one teacher handled this in a most delightful manner.

This teacher made a really large poster on good, heavy stock of a clown with an extra large open mouth (see **Figure 4-7**). Next, she took paper fasteners (the kind that you push through and then spread apart) and placed them through the poster at various intervals around the clown's lips until there were as many fastener ends showing as there were children in the class. Then she requisitioned a box of "metal-rimmed key tags with string." These were round, heavy-paper disks, rimmed in metal with a hole in each one, through which ran a loop of string. On each tag she wrote the name of a child in the class. This could also be done by cutting tags from stiff paper (oaktag) and attaching string through a hole you had punched yourself.

Now she was ready. On any given day, if a child wanted to buy lunch, he or she got the appropriate tag (this teacher kept them in a cup on her desk, but they could be stored in any convenient place) and looped the string over one of the studs on the clown's lips. This happened as the children arrived for school, so no class time was wasted. When all were in attendance, the teacher counted the disks that remained in the cup, subtracted this from the total number in class, and had her lunch count.

The lunches were delivered to the classroom in this particular situation, and each child who had ordered retrieved his or her tag from the clown's lips, presented it to the teacher, got a lunch, and the tag was placed back in the cup. By the time the lunches had been distributed, everything was set up for the following day.

This seems to us a very clever and charming way of handling this situation on an elementary level.

COLLECTING MONEY (I)

As teachers, we all have gone through the process of collecting money from our class for something or other. In the next discussion, we'll talk about collecting money for the special event, but right now let's talk about those common and frequent collections for such things as snacks, lunch money, student book clubs, and the like.

One way to handle it in a time-efficient manner and instill some responsibility in your students at the same time is to assign the task to student bankers. Choose two students for the task. They receive a sheet with the names of the children in the class. As a student hands in money, one banker takes it, counts it, and checks off the student's name. The other banker counts the money again and makes out the receipt shown in **Figure 4-8**.

When the collection for a particular day has been completed, the sheet and the money are turned in to the teacher.

If you wish, you can assign this task to different students each week, each month or each marking period as you deem appropriate. It is very good experience for them, and with two people doing it and cross-checking each other, it has proven to be very accurate as well. Moreover, the receipt given out to the student who pays has settled more than one argument about who did or did not hand in money.

You might want to set up a special time each day for the collection process such as before school, during homeroom, at the end of recess or at any time when the activity won't be disturbing your class or be inconvenient for you.

This process works well from upper elementary right through secondary grades. It will save you a great deal of time and trouble while teaching a valuable lesson to your students as well.

COLLECTING MONEY (II)

Collecting money for that "special project" is somewhat different than collecting money on a daily basis. We will illustrate by telling you about a class that was raising money for a class trip to Washington, D.C., but the technique used could be applied to any situation in which money is being collected for a special occasion.

The teacher used the poster shown in **Figure 4-9**. This is an outline of a student, colored to show him dressed in school colors. Down his front were drawn large buttons with dollar amounts beside each one. At the bottom was pasted a postcard of Washington, D.C., the ultimate destination of the class.

Now, this teacher found out that you can take pennies and place them into the tip of one of those long, thin balloons (they are called "airship" balloons), and the more pennies you place there, the longer the balloon will stretch. In fact, we were amazed when we saw how long it could stretch.

She took a red balloon and fastened it with a clip to the inside of the cutout mouth of the student portrayed on the poster. It hung down in front and became the character's tongue.

When the class reached one stage (indicated by a button on the poster), the teacher placed just enough pennies into the balloon that it stretched down to the first button. When the next stage was reached, more pennies enabled the tongue to hang down to the second button. So it went, until the character's tongue was touching the postcard of Washington, and the class had achieved its goal.

Since one's "tongue hanging out" is a fairly universal symbol of really desiring something, this was not only appropriate, but it proved highly motivational for the class.

The teacher who did this claimed that she had to do very little prodding or reminding of students once this poster was in use. That saved her and the class some time and effort, and the acclamation she received from parents and her colleagues for this unique idea was pretty nice too.

THE CLASSROOM INVENTORY (I)

Some teachers keep very neat desks with wide, clear spaces and all necessary utensils within easy reach. Others we know keep a desk that is continually piled high with papers, books, calendars and many other objects.

We once asked such a teacher how she knew where to find things. She replied that she knew where everything was and could locate any given object in seconds. That might have been true, but it did not apply to any other teacher who had to use her desk. Indeed, this teacher was once called at home in the middle of an attack of intestinal flu and asked where she had put her planbook, because no one could find it!

Which leads us to the classroom inventory. Simply put, this is a form such as that in **Figure 4-10**. Once filled out, it lists all the things in your classroom that you—or a teacher covering your class, a substitute teacher, or the school administration—would need.

In the column at the left, place the name of the article. There you would make entries such as planbook, marking book, seating charts, teacher's edition of a textbook, special folders, writing utensils, extra paper, art materials and so on. Place here anything that you feel might be needed by anyone when you're not present.

In the spaces to the right, place the location of each item. This might include phrases such as "teacher's desk, center drawer," "file cabinet, third drawer," "closet, top shelf, right." You place enough information here that someone looking for an item in your absence would have no trouble finding it.

We would suggest filing this form with the main office or your department chairpersons so that it will always be handy should the need arise.

The use of this relatively simple form can save a great deal of lost time and frustration for you and the entire school. What's more, you won't be called from your sick bed at home to be asked where you hid the teacher's edition of the reading book, either—and that's a real plus!

THE CLASSROOM INVENTORY (II)

Obviously, it is good to know when you are running low on an item so that you can replenish the supply before you run out. To pass out books to a class, only to find that you are three short, or to take out the construction paper for a project and find that you are down to your last six sheets, all of them deep purple, is not only frustrating but time-consuming. Your only options are to try to "borrow" the needed materials or quickly modify the activity.

Two methods have worked in keeping track of the classroom inventory and allowing the teacher to know the status of classroom supplies. The first one involves students, while the second is primarily for the teacher.

One teacher made his students into counters. They received titles such as Counter of the Reading Books, Counter of the Writing Paper and Counter of Classroom Rulers. The task assigned each student was exactly what the title implied. The Counter of the Reading Books was to count the reading books each day and report to the teacher if the number fell below a certain amount that the teacher had told him.

This teacher had virtually every student in the room responsible for counting something. One benefit was that whenever the teacher needed a count, there it was. Also, perhaps because a daily count was being kept, lost materials were reduced significantly.

A second method of keeping a running inventory by yourself is to group all your materials in bundles of 10. Put 10 pencils or 10 rulers together and place a rubber band around them; when stacking books, place 10 one way and 10 in the opposite direction; 10 classroom scissors can be joined by a plastic bag "twister" through the thumb holes. You don't have to do this with reams of paper or sealed packages of index cards or particularly large objects.

Now, almost at a glance, you can keep a running total of your supplies. Counted in units of 10, that stack of books can be totaled in three seconds. Are you running low on pencils? A quick look and count of the packages in your drawer will tell you at once. In short, just by looking, you can approximate the status of your supplies in a fraction of the time you would need if you were to count each piece.

Of course, you might want to combine these methods, but that's up to you. Whichever you care to try, here's hoping you never run short!

LOCATING RECORDS WHEN NEEDED

In the light of a tragedy that had happened in a nearby school district, a group of teachers were discussing the need to take certain records with them when they had to exit the building quickly as in an evacuation.

As a result of their brainstorming, each teacher made up a special emergency pack, which was kept in a file cabinet or drawer where the teacher could get at it instantly. It was labeled Emergency Record Pack as in **Figure 4-11**.

The pack was nothing more than a 9×12-inch manila clasp envelope with the label in **Figure 4-11** taped on the front. Inside the envelope these teachers placed a copy of the class lists with home and emergency telephone numbers, a small first aid kit, a small mechanical pencil, a note pad, four quarters, and a whistle. These items were listed in the appropriate spaces on the label and were checked periodically to see that all information was current.

Now, should an emergency occur in which the school had to be evacuated fast, you only have to grab the Emergency Record Pack to have everything you need in the event the emergency is not a drill but the real thing. For one thing, you have the physical necessities you will need (a whistle to call the class together, materials for writing messages; money for an outside phone call). You also have your records, which will not only tell you who may or may not be missing from the group but also give you the telephone numbers to contact for emergency action.

You would, of course, determine for yourself the exact nature of the materials going into the pack and list those accordingly on the label.

RECORDKEEPING CHECKLIST

If there were but one time-management caution about recordkeeping that we could give you, it would be this: Don't allow yourself to get behind your recordkeeping, or it will bury you. One record not completed this week means two for you to do next week or four for you at the end of the month. Multiply that by the number of records you have to complete each day, week, month or marking period, and you have some idea of the paper avalanche waiting to fall.

Teachers finding themselves in that position had better be reconciled to a red-eyed weekend of nothing but paperwork, paperwork, paperwork!

You keep on top of your recordkeeping by keeping track of your records. Toward this end, the checklist in **Figure 4-12** will be a great help. Here's how you use it. You fill in the information at the top and in the spaces in the left-hand column, you list the records, forms and reports that you must complete, turn in, or work on within the given time frame. In the appropriate space you place the date or dates on which the form or record is due and to whom it is going. You do this the moment you receive the form or report notice and keep it with this checklist. You now have everything in one place, you know when and to whom it is due and you have a good idea of the time frame left for you to do it.

Now the minute you complete that form or that report, record in the appropriate boxes the time finished and the date you sent it out.

This checklist will help you keep track of your recordkeeping chores. At a glance, you will be able to see what you are required to do, what you have done, and what yet remains to do. Keeping on top of your recordkeeping like this will ensure that nothing will pile up or come as an unwelcome surprise to you.

If we can keep ahead of our recordkeeping tasks, we have a good portion of the battle already won.

Teacher:_____ Date:_____

OPENING DAY INFORMATION

As we go through each of the following forms and materials, please check it off when it has been explained. When we are finished, please sign the statement at the bottom. This sheet will be collected at the end of this class.

( ) PTA Information   ( ) Locker Assignment
( ) Insurance Form   ( ) Locker Key/Combination
( ) Attendance Data Form   ( ) Emergency Cards
( ) Student Handbook   ( ) Student Information Card
( ) Class Requirements   ( ) Letter to Parents
( ) Class Rules   ( ) Federal Lunch Form

I have received and had explained to me all of the above forms.

Student:_____ Date:_____

Figure 4-1
Opening Day Information Checklist

Date: _____

Dear _____,

Please excuse this form letter; I'm certain you understand how hectic and time-consuming the opening of school can be.

Along with this letter comes an index card which your child made out in class today. This is information that makes it easier for me to contact you during the year and handle any special situations that may arise.

Would you please check it for accuracy? If there is anything you think I should know or that you wish me to know about your child, please indicate this on the back of the card. In either case, could you please sign it so I'll know that all the information is correct and up to date.

Thank you for your cooperation, and I look forward to meeting you soon.

Yours sincerely,

Figure 4-2
Student Information Check

Teacher:_____ Room:_____

Class/Section:_____ For the Month of:_____

Name of   Date
Student

☑ = Present   A = Absent   T = Tardy

Figure 4-3
Classroom Attendance Form

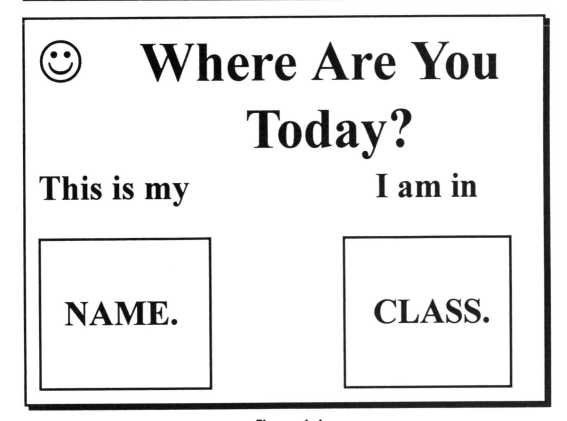

Figure 4-4
Classroom Attendance Poster

Teacher:_____ School Year:_____
Subject:_____ Period:_____ Class:_____
Marking Period:_____ From:_____ To:_____

TEST AND QUIZ RESULTS

Test Date and Subject Matter	Avg.	Quiz Date and Subject Matter	Avg.

Student:

Figure 4-5
Test and Quiz Record Sheet

Teacher:_____ Date:_____

Class/Section:_____

Question: _____

_____

_____

TO STUDENTS: Please place your INITIALS in the correct box to
indicate your choice.

Class List:	Yes	No

Figure 4-6
Class All-Purpose Count Sheet

Figure 4-7
Lunch Count Clown Poster

Teacher:_____

Date:_____

*Received of:*_____

*the Amount of:*_____

*for:*_____

_____

*Received by:*_____

Figure 4-8
Money Collection Receipt

Figure 4-9
Money Collection Poster

CLASSROOM INVENTORY

Teacher:_____

Grade & Subject:_____

For Room:_____ **School Year:**_____

Item:	Location:

Special Information:

_____

_____

_____

_____

_____

Figure 4-10
Classroom Inventory Form

Emergency Record Pack

This packet contains the following:

_____

_____

_____

_____

_____

_____

_____

_____

_____

Figure 4-11
Emergency Record Pack

RECORDKEEPING CHECKLIST

Teacher:_____

Grade & Subject:_____

For the Time Period from _____ to _____

Report:	Date Due:	Send Report To:	Finished:	Sent:

Special Notes:

Figure 4-12
Recordkeeping Checklist

MANAGING STUDENT/TEACHER INTERACTIONS

Student/teacher interaction is what teaching is all about—someone to impart knowledge and someone else to take it in. This simple truth lies at the foundation of all we do as teachers. It is that interaction between you and your students that stirs souls, opens eyes, and frees minds.

That is not to say that this interaction is always free from problems. Often, it is a frustrating, sometimes apparently thankless, frequently time-consuming process that can try our strength and our patience. In this section, let's examine some ways in which teachers have worked effectively within this time-honored relationship.

DEALING WITH THE TOTAL PAPER LOAD (I)

The paper load that we face each week as teachers has been described as "a paper tiger that threatens to devour us all." Few teachers would argue over that description. Certainly, we realize the fearsome awe of that stack of papers pressing down upon us. We must find ways to tame that tiger, or it will certainly tame us.

Let's investigate some methods for effectively managing the time we spend on the total paperwork load.

First, we can, wherever possible, use student aides to handle much of the paperwork. Section 2 provided insights into the use of aides in dealing with homework, particularly Figures 2-10 and 2-11, and in Section 4, Figure 4-6 was presented in connection with the use of student aides for doing much of the time-consuming tasks related to student paperwork. Certainly, for much of the daily routine, properly supervised student aides can really help us cope effectively with the paper onslaught.

The most time-efficient way of handling the student papers that cannot be handled by student aides (or, those that you do not wish handled by them) is to make certain that you do not wall yourself into a corner using paper bricks.

One teacher we know gave his students a composition each week, which he dutifully corrected. He gave the composition every Friday, and every Friday, he brought home 135 compositions to correct over the weekend. He spent his entire Saturday correcting student written work.

How much easier it would have been had he staggered that assignment as indicated in **Figure 5-1**. He still has his one composition per week, and his students still have the benefit of it, but now he has only 20-odd papers to correct at one time instead of 135. Judiciously planned, he could get them done during school time in his professional or planning period or even on his hall-duty assignment. What a pleasure to have your Saturday free!

With proper planning and taking advantage of the resources about us, if we can't cut down on the amount of paper, we can surely manage the time spent on it to our advantage.

DEALING WITH THE TOTAL PAPER LOAD (II)

How much of a paper load is too much? That's a good question, but sometimes the answer isn't very obvious. Certainly, if you are correcting close to 100 papers each day (and, we knew a teacher who did), you are doing too much. The question still remains, however. How much is too much?

The form in **Figure 5-2** can help you determine the answer to that question as applied to your teaching and your classes. As you can see, it is rather self-explanatory, so let's just look at some of its major points.

To get the most out of this form, you must be honest and accurate. We would suggest taking your figures from the last full week of class you taught, provided it wasn't the beginning or last week of school. Go through your planbook and marking book and get exact answers as much as possible. Be accurate with your data.

Under Assignment, list everything you did during that week that required you to handle a student paper. Do you have five classes of 25 students each? Did you get homework from them all on one day? That's 125 papers. Place that number under the day you handled them. The same goes for tests, quizzes, journals, compositions, reaction papers and the like. If *you* handled a piece of paper, record it.

When you have determined your Average Daily Paper Load, remember that the interpretation of that figure that we have included at the bottom of the form is, in the final analysis, just an opinion. It is you who will have to live with your decision. It is you who best know your class and your own capabilities.

Finally, go back over the individual sources of paper. Perhaps one area suddenly stands out as excessive. Are you handling too much homework? Perhaps you would like to reread Section 2 of this book for some ideas on how to cut down the time spent in this area and more efficiently manage the time you do spend. Are the student journals you assigned now taking over your life? See the next discussion for suggestions on cutting time spent there.

In short, first you must know that your paper load is unreasonable, and you must see in black and white where the problem area lies. Then you can use this book, ask a veteran master teacher or make up a method of your own. Whatever your course of action, help is available, and you are on your way to managing that massive paper load (and your professional time) more effectively and efficiently.

CORRECTING OF STUDENT WRITTEN WORK (I)

Many teachers believe that students should write every day. Our purpose here is not to get into such things as journal writing or reaction papers, because you know the value of them. Rather, let us share with you a method that will greatly reduce the time you have to spend correcting that daily written work should you decide to give it.

Figure 5-3 represents a section of a reaction paper that the teacher assigned on a daily basis. The students are given a certain amount of time to write freely. Then the paper is either handed in, or first discussed and then given in. Before passing in the paper, however, the student first circles five consecutive lines of writing. It is understood that these five lines are the only part that the teacher will read or correct.

Remember, we are not speaking here of a major composition that will count as a percentage of a final grade. Rather, we are talking of the day-to-day writing that a class might do in order to gain facility in writing and putting ideas down on paper.

In having the student circle five lines (or however many you may choose) and correcting only those, you are giving individual attention to each student, gaining insight into student progress and helping each child develop writing skills *in a fraction of the time* that it would take to go over each paper fully.

Remember, you don't have to drink a gallon of milk to tell if it's fresh; a sip will do. Similarly, this representative sampling will allow you to assess the progress and status of your class while saving you much time in correcting this type of student written work.

CORRECTING OF STUDENT WRITTEN WORK (II)

In spite of all the techniques and methods and shuffling of paper, you eventually will have to sit down with that red or blue or green pencil in your hand, get yourself a cup of coffee, put your feet up—and actually correct that stack of papers that you took from your desk as you left school this afternoon. It will help if we share some insights into the process gleaned from those who have had long experience with it.

First, never correct a paper that is incomplete or sloppily done. Papers of this sort should be returned to the student who is told that the paper will be recorded as missing until such time as it comes back in a condition favorable for correction. Don't waste time over something that the student obviously didn't take the time to do properly in the first place.

Next, group your papers in units of 10 and take a short break after each unit. If you have 40 papers, make four packages of 10 and bind each with a paper clip. As you finish one bunch, get up, stretch, take a walk around the room or the house. Break the routine of paper correction, and you will come back to it refreshed and ready to go on to the next set of ten.

Then, if your eyes start to bother you or your vision goes blurry, stop correcting immediately and see your eye doctor. Nothing could justify ruining your sight over the correction of papers. Make certain that your eyes are checked, that you wear the proper glasses if you have to and that you do not sacrifice your health for the correction of student papers.

Finally, you might want to record grades *as you correct* rather than going through the entire stack after you have finished. A simple sheet as in **Figure 5-4** would suffice. It can be made up by cutting out the list of names from your class roster and pasting them over the space for names on the form. Then the whole thing can be copied as many times as you wish. If you are sitting in a chair correcting a stack of papers, this small sheet can be handled far more easily than a large marking book. Using this method, you handle the papers once, and that's it.

Any or all of these, while hardly making paper correction into a holiday sport, will help the process go a little smoother and easier.

AVOIDING ARGUMENTS OVER POOR GRADES

We have had some students over the years who could really argue about their grades. Indeed, we have also had some parents who could really argue over their children's grades as well. Sometimes, the arguments could get fairly heated. Of course, we had the records of test and quiz results as well as evidence of homework and assignments missed or undone, but the process was always an involved one that took quite some time.

Finally, a colleague introduced us to the sheet seen in **Figure 5-5**. The teacher who originally used this passed out one to each member of the class just prior to report cards being released. Since this teacher required that students keep *all* returned papers for an entire marking period, they should be able to fill out the sheet without difficulty.

The math involved can be done by each student, and the note at the bottom of the form is self-explanatory and precludes arguments from that sector. In the time she used this, the teacher reported that the vast majority of her students were able to determine their marking period grades *exactly*.

If there are still arguments, the first thing to be checked is that the student put down the correct grades and homework assignments done and undone (even the best of students may engage in selective memory from time to time). Most disputes are quickly settled then and there.

Indeed, many a potential argument will never materialize as the student discovers the hard facts of his or her class grades justifies the teacher's assessment rather than the student's academic fantasy.

CHOOSING STUDENTS TO WORK IN GROUPS

Virtually every teacher does group work from time to time. There are many benefits to it, including the fact that students learn to work together and often learn from each other in the process. Unfortunately, there are some drawbacks as well.

"I don't want to work with a girl!" exclaims a boy. "I won't work with a boy!" echoes a girl. "Buddy Cravitts hates me," another informs you, "and I won't work with him!" If you were to listen to the requirements set by the students in your class for working in groups with each other, you could well spend a month selecting groups for a two-day project!

Let us tell you how one teacher saves time and argument in the selection of students to work in groups.

First, he passes out the sheet in **Figure 5-6**. Please note several things about this paper. First, it is a given that all students will work in groups; no one has the option of not working. Next, there is a set number of people to be in the group, no more and no less. Third, the composition of the group is clearly defined—no all-boy or all-girl groups are allowed. Finally, students have a guided choice of the people with whom they will work.

Before students begin to work on these sheets, the teacher explains what was just detailed in the previous paragraph. He explains that everyone must be included along the guidelines of the sheet. He further tells them that, if there are duplicates such as a person on two lists, then that group will be reassigned according to the teacher's wishes. He gives his class 10 minutes of class time to talk and make their own arrangements before he calls the class to order and directs them to fill out the sheet.

When these sheets are completed and turned in, student aides check them to ensure continuity and to see to it that all directions have been followed. If there is a discrepancy—a child not included, incorrect balance, known enemies together— they are reported to the teacher who makes adjustments according to his knowledge of the class. Finally, each group is listed by the student aides and posted on the bulletin board for the next day.

Given the preparation of the class and the printed requirements for groups, this teacher reports that only infrequently must he "amend" the selections. He also tells us that the groups work in much closer harmony than the ones he used to select for his students. There is a feeling among the students that they had a free choice of the people in their group, yet the teacher was satisfied that he had established proper group dynamics for his class.

If you can take a few minutes to establish groups that don't grumble, don't complain, and work together productively, then you have benefitted from it and so have your students.

CHOOSING STUDENTS TO ANSWER QUESTIONS

We made a discovery one day after watching ourselves on videotape, and for us it was shocking. We found that we were calling on the same kids most of the time. It was not our intention to do this; we would have strongly advised others against it, but there were some kids who always had an answer, and we had been calling on them almost exclusively. Albeit subconsciously, we had allowed some kids to go without answering for up to a month, while others got called every day. When this was brought to our attention, we were shocked and humbled, especially since we had no one to blame but ourselves.

One way you could handle that situation would be to use a form as in **Figure 5-7**. You list the names of the people in your class (or paste in the names from a copied class list) and check off a space every time you call on a student. In this way you could keep track of who had and *had not* been called to answer. (See also the following discussions in this section, "Avoiding Gender Bias" and "Assessing Needs for Interaction.")

An even better way that we found was to let your students do the choosing. You call on your first student to answer; let's say her name is Andrea. Whatever answer Andrea may give, you continue with the class until it becomes time for the next question to be answered. Now, you call on Andrea again, and this time Andrea selects the next student to answer, let's say Carl. Carl answers, and when it comes time for the next question, you go back to Carl who selects the person who is going to answer next. In short, the student who answered previously selects the student to answer next.

Add to this the rule (explained to the class, of course) that no student may be called a second time until everybody has answered, and you have a classroom where *everybody* answers *every day*. If you have enough questions to ask, you might even have everyone in class answering two or three times each day.

With this method, you don't have to take the time to choose anyone but the first student to answer, and you know for a certainty that everyone will be getting a chance to answer and learn. Ask the question *before* you go to the student to find out who will answer, and the whole class will stay alert.

From personal experience, we assure you that this works extremely well once the class has learned the process and taken it to heart.

AVOIDING GENDER BIAS

When we were children, sitting on the other side of the desk we always enjoyed being assigned work tasks by the teacher. Washing blackboards (once a week we'd rub lemon oil into them; we can still remember the smell), passing out books, opening windows and the like were pleasant breaks in the routine, and the air was always filled with hands when the teacher requested a volunteer. You did not volunteer for everything, however, because it was clearly understood that there were some tasks that were reserved for boys and some for girls, and that line was never crossed. A girl *never* got to move books from one place to another, because that was a boy's task; a boy *did not* clean the play corner, because that was reserved for girls.

That may be the way it was, but times have changed. Those gender-based stereotypes simply no longer apply in today's society, nor should they have any place in our public schools. Certainly, most of us realize that the criteria for the assignment of a task should be the ability of the individual to complete the task and *not* whether the student is male or female.

A number of teachers have shared with us their techniques for avoiding this gender bias in the assignment of classroom tasks. Let's look at some of them.

One teacher has a paperweight with labels stuck on the top and bottom on which she has written "boy" and "girl" respectively. When she needs somebody for a task, she looks at the uppermost label and picks a girl or boy accordingly. Then, she turns the paperweight over, and it is ready to direct her next selection. In this manner, she claims, boys and girls are equally alternated, and she doesn't have to keep track of who was chosen last.

Another teacher uses the form in **Figure 5-8**. He lists the girls on one side and the boys on the other. Each time he chooses someone for a task, he places a check next to the name. In this way, he told us, he can make certain that he is choosing equitably, and he can also see if he is favoring one or two students above others and make an instant correction should the need arise. (See also "Choosing Students to Answer Questions" and "Assessing Needs for Interaction" in this section.)

Still another teacher picks a student for a task, and that student chooses the next student to help or do another job. The only stipulation the teacher places on the student is that the student selected must be of the opposite gender. Thus, a boy may select any *girl* in the class, and a girl may select any *boy*. According to this teacher, it works out well.

Avoiding gender bias can be done quickly and efficiently, with your students reaping the benefits.

THE FIRST DAY OF THE SUBJECT

Earlier in Section Four, we discussed some techniques for handling the general administrative hubbub attendant to the first day of school. That was related to homeroom activities and the general information needed for the school itself. Now let's talk about that first day in *your* new class with *your* students.

On the first day of your subject, you are going to have to go through the "business" of getting the student information that you require and passing out textbooks. (See the beginning of Section Four.) If you are like us, you will also want a chance to observe your new students.

On the first day of our subject, students arrive to find a textbook on each desk and an index card with their name on it on top of each textbook. Once they have found their names and are sitting in those desks, they are automatically in the seating plan we have devised for them, and we immediately know the identity of each student.

We have them make out the information we require on the index cards, and print their names in the textbooks. Then we give them the sheet in **Figure 5-9**. They are required to fill out the entire form. While this is happening, we have the opportunity to call each one up to the desk to record the textbook number and get a personal and closer look at each student, perhaps exchanging a word or two as seems appropriate.

The sheet itself, we feel, is not mere busy work. It makes students think about the value of the subject, requires the formation of short-term goals and asks them to formulate those thoughts in writing.

We keep these forms in the file cabinet, because they can prove useful throughout the year. We have shown a failing student his own words and expectations. We have shared what a child wrote about what she did and did not hope to accomplish with a child's parents. We have used them to help a guidance counselor help a troubled student. Certainly, many uses will occur to you as well.

By the end of that first day of your subject, with just a little effort on your part, you will have accomplished quite a lot and learned a great deal about your students in the process.

GETTING THE MOST OUT OF DETENTION

We witnessed a detention once in which five students sat in a classroom after regular school hours. One was doing his homework, one had fallen asleep, another was daydreaming out the window and the last two were engaged in a heated discussion about the party at Tara's house last Saturday.

If this sounds more like a social club than a detention, it looked that way to us as well. Indeed, the teacher running that scene had better plan to spend more and more afternoons in that classroom, because occasions for detention are going to get more frequent in his class. That detention was no deterrent at all; it was a pleasant afternoon with friends!

When a teacher we know holds detention, it might be after school, or it might be for half an hour before school starts in the morning. She has found that the morning detention is often far more effective, since students have to rise early and often have to have their parents bring them to school. Whatever the time, when the child steps into the room for detention, she presents the student with the sheet in **Figure 5-10**.

As you can see, filling out this sheet will take an average student the full detention period. During that time, the teacher checks occasionally to see that the work is being done. The rest of the time she spends doing her own work. By the end of the detention period, she has gotten some schoolwork done, the student has been made to think and been kept busy and working all period long, and there has been no "social club" atmosphere. Detention, in the future, will be something to be avoided rather than joked about. Moreover, the students' answers may now be kept for possible future use.

What makes a student do all that work during the detention period? Well, we are certain that you noticed the last line on the sheet. The kids notice it, too!

Keep a detention such as this, and you'll soon find that you are not staying nearly as often as you were for disciplinary reasons, and the discipline in your classroom will have improved as well.

SUPERVISING THE PLAYGROUND

If you are supervising your own class on the playground, it is difficult but not an impossible task. But if you are supervising four or five classes on the playground by yourself, you have a job and a half on your hands. Indeed, the more children on the playground, the more playground monitors there should be. Most schools recognize this fact.

Even with several teachers on post, however, it is a far from easy task. Something happens at one end of the area and you rush there, only to find the culprits vanished, and an uproar issuing from the section you just left. It can be most frustrating.

Here is how one group of playground monitors solved that problem.

To illustrate, let's say that there were four monitors on duty. They made a rough sketch of the playground area and divided it into four sections. This is seen in **Figure 5-11**. Then, one teacher was assigned or volunteered to cover *one* of those areas. Each agreed to rotate into a new area each month to keep alert.

If something happened in one teacher's section, that teacher and only that teacher, took care of it. For something large, such as a fight involving several students, the teacher could always signal for help and the others would come immediately, but they did not leave their posts unless specifically asked. In this way, every inch of that playground was covered by supervision at virtually all times, and no longer could students play "divide and conquer" with the playground monitors.

Naturally, you would divide your playground area in proportion to the number of supervisors you had available during that playground period. The teachers involved found this an excellent way to quickly and efficiently cover the larger area with total supervision.

WORKING IN AN EXTRACURRICULAR ACTIVITY

If you have ever worked with or been an advisor to an extracurricular activity, particularly one in which a number of students have been involved, you know the frustration that can often result. Here is a method that not only saves a great deal of time but also makes life much smoother for the activity's advisor.

First, create (or guide your students to manufacture) a *member packet* for each student who joins the extracurricular activity. This packet should contain a number of items. There should be an index card with whatever data a member of the activity should know, such as deadlines for publication or the activity's office phone number, its mailing address and the like. There should be blank forms that members may need to use often such as permission slips for trips, passes to and from class, and so forth. There should be an activity schedule and any other materials (such as a membership card or special club button) that the advisor can imagine a member will want or need.

Now prepare an *advisor's packet* which should contain a list of all members with data such as homeroom numbers, home telephone numbers, student schedules and so on. If the activity is the kind that has students out of class from time to time (forensics, for example), perhaps you will want a master class schedule to ensure that students aren't out of the same periods all the time. If it's the type of activity that takes students out of school, then you might want to include extra bus passes, request for transportation forms, trip itinerary forms and the like. Include everything you need as the advisor.

When a student becomes a member of the activity, he or she is given a member packet. Thereafter, the student is responsible for having access to this packet at all times. For example, when they know that a trip is coming up (a debate at a school in another district, let's say), they become responsible for getting a permission slip from their packet and having it filled out and returned. When they get down to the next to last of *anything*, they are to go to the advisor or student aide in charge and get a refill.

As advisor, you keep your "master" packet with your other records where you can find and use it as needed.

This method will not solve all of your extracurricular problems, but it will help things go a great deal smoother.

TALKING WITH STUDENTS

One of the most enjoyable things about teaching is talking with our students. So much can be learned, and we can do so much good talking one-on-one to a student. The personal contact of a teacher-student conversation simply cannot be matched in a formal classroom setup.

The process is not without problems, however. One teacher always had students come to her at the end of class to talk about what they had discussed that day. She enjoyed the interaction with her pupils until the principal spoke to her one day about complaints from other teachers that her students were continually coming in late for the next class.

Let's look at what some teachers have done to manage the time used for talking to students.

One teacher who found that students were always staying after the lesson to ask questions solved the problem by ending his class three minutes before the official bell. Some students began their homework, some students talked quietly with their friends, and some students came to the teacher to talk. No student was late to the next class.

Another teacher traditionally came in a good half-hour before the scheduled start of the school day. This teacher made it known that she would be available at that time for any student who wanted to talk about anything. Students could come to her at any time during the day to express a desire to talk, and she would give them a pass allowing them to get into the building early and come up to her room. In this way, she was able to speak to students in the relative quiet and privacy of a prestudent school. She claims that there was much accomplished during that early-morning half-hour that helped her students greatly.

Still another teacher was assigned library duty as part of his schedule. If a child really needed to talk to him, this teacher would do a little "behind the scenes" work, and see if he could get the student's teacher to send the student to the library, even for a few moments, during the time that he was on duty there. Most colleagues, he reports, were cooperative if there seemed to be a real need on the part of the student. This teacher did the same thing the following year when he was assigned hall duty.

So, here are three ways in which you can get to talk face to face with your students without interfering with the process of education in the school or with another teacher's class. The benefits to your students and to you are truly outstanding.

ASSESSING NEEDS FOR INTERACTION

As teachers, we realize that we are teaching every child in the class, and we like to make certain that we interact with each and every student. The phrase *quality time* has almost become a cliché, but that is what we would all like to have with every student in our class.

It doesn't always work out that way. As young teachers, we once came across a student's name on a class list. We were certain a mistake had been made, because not only was the name unfamiliar, but we could place no face with it at all. Much to our chagrin, we found that the boy was, indeed, our student. He was a painfully shy boy who sat in the back of class, never caused any trouble, never raised his eyes or his head, never asked questions, and never volunteered. Sadly, we realized that we had ignored the child completely and had not interacted with him for the entire marking period.

Of course, we tried to remedy that injustice on our part, but it really set us to thinking. A short time later, we fashioned the chart in **Figure 5-12**. We kept this form in the marking book, which was always open on our desk. With the class list down one side, it was an easy matter that soon became habitual to place a check after a child's name whenever we interacted with him or her. This did not mean merely asking a question, but it could include such things as assigning a task, talking to the child after class or even just smiling or winking at the child.

At the end of each week (or whatever time period you choose), we looked at the chart and could instantly see those with whom we had interacted and, more importantly, those with whom we had *not*. Thereafter, special effort could be made to give greater attention where it was needed. Never again would there be a student who could sit in the back with his head down and go unnoticed. (See also "Choosing Students to Answer Questions" and "Avoiding Gender Bias" Earlier in this section.)

We found this a remarkably simple and effective way of assessing the need for interaction with our students. After a few days, it became all but automatic, proving a great help in increasing the interactive, quality time we spend with our students.

TEACHER TIME-MANAGEMENT CALENDAR

We have personally used a most simple expedient for years to save a good deal of trouble in managing our time in teaching. Let's take a look at it, and show you how you can use it to help manage your time.

The squares in **Figure 5-13** are arranged in such a manner that you could write in the dates of any calendar month of the year and make it into a calendar for that month. The squares are big and easily accessible for jotting down notes.

Copy this form onto *one end* of a "legal size" sheet of paper (8.5×14 inches). Fill in all that is needed to make it a calendar for the month you want. Then, with it flat on the desk, take the bottom edge of the legal size sheet and fold up about one-third of it. Staple the edges together, and you now have a calendar for the month with a fair-sized pocket underneath it. This can be kept in your marking book or desk, or it can even be posted on a bulletin board.

There is enough space to write down the dates and times of conferences, faculty and departmental meetings, special deadlines and more—anything you need to be reminded of for effective time management. Now, if a form is involved, such as an itinerary, booklist, record or form that goes with the meeting you noted on the calendar, fold it and place it in the pocket below the calendar.

Now, not only can you manage your time more efficiently due to the wide view of time afforded you, but you have just one place to go to find any materials you will need for that event, whatever it may be. This alone will save you much time searching desks and file cabinets for needed papers.

Eventually, we backed each one on construction paper to make it firmer, and if this helps you as it has us, you might want to do that as well.

This is a good start toward effectively managing your educational interactions.

Mon.	Tues.	Wed.	Thurs.	Fri.
COMP	class	class	class	class
class	**COMP**	class	class	class
class	class	**COMP**	class	class
class	class	class	**COMP**	class
class	class	class	class	**COMP**

Figure 5-1
Paper-Load Distribution Schedule

Name:_____

Information for the five-day period from _____ to _____.

AVERAGE DAILY PAPER LOAD

Assignment	Day 1	Day 2	Day 3	Day 4	Day 5	Total
Total Number of Papers						
Average Daily Paper Load (divide Total No. by 5)						

Possible Analysis:

1 - 20 = possibly too little   51 - 100 = on the heavy side

21 - 50 = about average   101 + = possibly too much

Figure 5-2
Paper-Load Evaluation Form

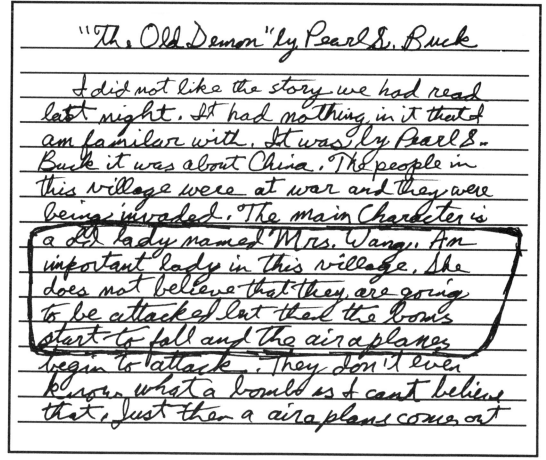

Figure 5-3
Written Work Sample

Class:_____ From:_____ To:_____

UNIT TEST RECORD

Student (date)	Unit 1	Unit 2	Unit 3	Unit 4	Unit 5	Unit 6

Figure 5-4
Written Work Correction Record

Name:_____ Marking Period:_____

MARKING PERIOD GRADE ANALYSIS

No. of Homeworks Assigned: ____ No. Satisfactorily Completed: ____
(missing or poorly done homework affects your marking period grade)

TEST grades: _____ Average:_____
(add test grades together and divide by the number of tests)

QUIZ grades:_____ Average:_____
(add quiz grades together and divide by the number of quizzes)

WRITTEN
WORK:_____ Average:_____
(add grades on written work and divide by the number of assignments)

MAIN AVERAGE (add averages; divide by 3): _____

POINTS TO REMEMBER:
       Missing or undone homework will lower your grade.
       How you perform in class affects your grade. It is the teacher's job
and responsibility to determine whether or not you are performing up to
your abilities. This determination is based upon the teacher's observa-
tions and experience, and it can raise or lower your grade.

Figure 5-5
Marking Period Grade Analysis

Your Name:_____ Date:_____

You must work in a group. This sheet will help to make up the group in which you work. Please take time and thought to fill it out.

REMEMBER: Four and ONLY FOUR people to a group.
                      Two boys and two girls to each group.
                      Choose people with whom you can WORK.
                      Include YOUR OWN NAME in the group.

Boys:

1. _____
2. _____
Alternate:_____

Girls:

1. _____
2. _____
Alternate:_____

Figure 5-6
Group Formation Analysis Form

Class: _____   **From:**_____   **To:**_____

Student   **Called Upon**

_____   ( ) ( ) ( ) ( ) ( ) ( ) ( ) ( ) ( ) ( ) ( )

_____   ( ) ( ) ( ) ( ) ( ) ( ) ( ) ( ) ( ) ( ) ( )

_____   ( ) ( ) ( ) ( ) ( ) ( ) ( ) ( ) ( ) ( ) ( )

_____   ( ) ( ) ( ) ( ) ( ) ( ) ( ) ( ) ( ) ( ) ( )

_____   ( ) ( ) ( ) ( ) ( ) ( ) ( ) ( ) ( ) ( ) ( )

_____   ( ) ( ) ( ) ( ) ( ) ( ) ( ) ( ) ( ) ( ) ( )

_____   ( ) ( ) ( ) ( ) ( ) ( ) ( ) ( ) ( ) ( ) ( )

_____   ( ) ( ) ( ) ( ) ( ) ( ) ( ) ( ) ( ) ( ) ( )

_____   ( ) ( ) ( ) ( ) ( ) ( ) ( ) ( ) ( ) ( ) ( )

_____   ( ) ( ) ( ) ( ) ( ) ( ) ( ) ( ) ( ) ( ) ( )

_____   ( ) ( ) ( ) ( ) ( ) ( ) ( ) ( ) ( ) ( ) ( )

_____   ( ) ( ) ( ) ( ) ( ) ( ) ( ) ( ) ( ) ( ) ( )

_____   ( ) ( ) ( ) ( ) ( ) ( ) ( ) ( ) ( ) ( ) ( )

_____   ( ) ( ) ( ) ( ) ( ) ( ) ( ) ( ) ( ) ( ) ( )

Figure 5-7
Student Participation Log

Class: _____ From: _____ To: _____

Boys   Girls

_____( ) ( ) ( ) ( ) ( ) ( )   _____( ) ( ) ( ) ( ) ( ) ( )

_____( ) ( ) ( ) ( ) ( ) ( )   _____( ) ( ) ( ) ( ) ( ) ( )

_____( ) ( ) ( ) ( ) ( ) ( )   _____( ) ( ) ( ) ( ) ( ) ( )

_____( ) ( ) ( ) ( ) ( ) ( )   _____( ) ( ) ( ) ( ) ( ) ( )

_____( ) ( ) ( ) ( ) ( ) ( )   _____( ) ( ) ( ) ( ) ( ) ( )

_____( ) ( ) ( ) ( ) ( ) ( )   _____( ) ( ) ( ) ( ) ( ) ( )

_____( ) ( ) ( ) ( ) ( ) ( )   _____( ) ( ) ( ) ( ) ( ) ( )

_____( ) ( ) ( ) ( ) ( ) ( )   _____( ) ( ) ( ) ( ) ( ) ( )

_____( ) ( ) ( ) ( ) ( ) ( )   _____( ) ( ) ( ) ( ) ( ) ( )

_____( ) ( ) ( ) ( ) ( ) ( )   _____( ) ( ) ( ) ( ) ( ) ( )

_____( ) ( ) ( ) ( ) ( ) ( )   _____( ) ( ) ( ) ( ) ( ) ( )

_____( ) ( ) ( ) ( ) ( ) ( )   _____( ) ( ) ( ) ( ) ( ) ( )

_____( ) ( ) ( ) ( ) ( ) ( )   _____( ) ( ) ( ) ( ) ( ) ( )

_____( ) ( ) ( ) ( ) ( ) ( )   _____( ) ( ) ( ) ( ) ( ) ( )

_____( ) ( ) ( ) ( ) ( ) ( )   _____( ) ( ) ( ) ( ) ( ) ( )

Figure 5-8
Student Task Poster

Name:_____ Date:_____

Class:_____ Teacher:_____

Please answer all of the following questions in the space provided. Please use all of the space and leave nothing blank.

What do you expect to learn in here this year?

How well (grades) do you expect to do? Why?

Why is this subject necessary for your future?

How can you make certain that you do well in this class?

What do you, personally, hope to accomplish in here this year?

On back of this paper, tell me four things about yourself that will help me to teach you better.

Figure 5-9
Student Expectation Sheet

Name:_____ Date:_____

Class:_____

Please answer all questions fully. Use additional paper if necessary. Fill all the space given for an answer.

Why does a teacher assign detention?

What does a teacher get out of detention?

How can detention be a good thing for a student?

How can you avoid detention in the future?

Using the entire back of this paper, explain what you did that led to this detention. Leave nothing out. The entire back of this paper must be filled.

SPECIAL NOTE: If you do not complete this entire form by the end of the detention period, you will do the entire thing over in another detention.

Figure 5-10
Student Detention Analysis Sheet

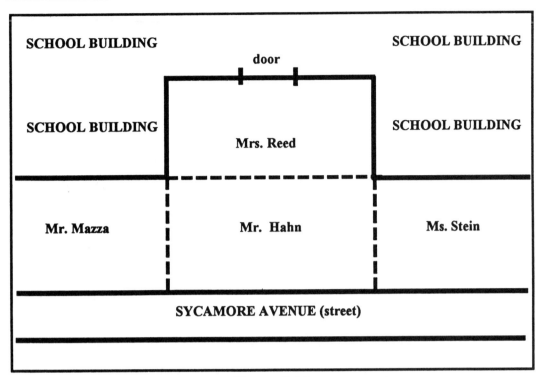

Figure 5-11
Playground Supervision Grid

Class:_____ From:_____ To:_____

Class List | Interaction

Figure 5-12
Student Interaction Chart

Figure 5-13
Teacher Time/Management Calendar

SAVING TIME IN YOUR ADMINISTRATIVE DUTIES

At times we act not so much as teachers as what may be termed "administrators." From answering our daily mail, preparing lesson plans, monitoring the halls and lunch rooms, to budgeting for the next school year, there are enough teaching-related yet nonteaching administrative duties each day to sap our time and energy.

Let's spend a little time looking at ways in which many teachers have dealt with these often time-consuming yet necessary tasks that are part and parcel of every teacher's day.

GETTING THE MOST OUT OF FACULTY AND DEPARTMENTAL MEETINGS

In spite of what some individuals will tell you, there is a definite need for faculty and departmental meetings. It is a place to quickly disseminate information to a large group, address common concerns, and learn about new methods, practices and policies.

In reality, they are also often dull, lifeless and too long, leaving teachers drooping in folding chairs or student desks. It is often quite difficult to concentrate all your energy on the speaker, particularly since you have just come from a long day with your students.

One innovative teacher changed that situation by publishing the list of questions in **Figure 6-1**. You will notice that this is not an agenda for the meeting (a departmental one in this case, but easily applied to a faculty meeting as well). Rather, this is a list of questions that *will be answered at the meeting*.

In effect, you have just taken the audience and turned them from *passive* to *active* listeners. Now they are no longer a group of people who have to be there. Now they are an active group who are listening for a purpose—to find the answers to those questions. Attentiveness and interest rise dramatically. (We were amazed; try it yourself.)

Of course, the questions to be answered will change according to the topics being covered, but our audience will no longer be spectators but participants, actively seeking—and getting the most out of—that faculty or departmental meeting.

DEALING WITH THE TOTAL MAIL LOAD

One of our colleagues once remarked that at least 174 trees must be cut down each year just to make the paper that filled her teacher mailbox from September through June. Of course, she was being facetious, but there are times when we look at that overstuffed cubbyhole in the main office with our name on it, and we wonder if our friend is really joking after all.

As teachers, we do seem to get an inordinate amount of mail. Besides the advertisements, letters of inquiry and other correspondence that comes via the postal service, we also find memos, forms for school use and other communications from within the building. Some have to be answered right now, while others are merely informational. It gets so that it can take a good five minutes just to sort out the mail and between 10 minutes and a half-hour to answer it all. We could really use a secretary.

A number of teachers in surrounding rooms felt the same way; so we formed our own "mail service." Four of us were involved and each of us took a week at a time. For the assigned week, one teacher acted as secretary to the group. This teacher agreed to come in a little early for that week and pick up the mail for all of us, keeping it separate, of course. He or she would then separate each teacher's mail into advertising, school memos, immediate attention, personal, and FYI (for your information). Each group would be rubber-banded, labeled with a self-adhesive memo sheet and placed on the appropriate teacher's desk.

The four of us found it an ideal situation. Our one week per month of coming in a trifle early and sorting the mail was more than repaid by the three weeks of having the mail on our desks, already sorted and ready to be handled, when we arrived at our rooms.

We did this among ourselves, because we did not feel that it was circumspect to allow students to handle mail that might, at times, contain sensitive material.

It saved us some time and effort, while being a bright spot that added positively to the school day.

DEALING WITH ADVERTISING BROCHURES

One of the many things that comes in the mail is the advertising brochure. In fact, they come with amazing frequency. They advertise special activities, books, book clubs, field trips, teaching aids, locally offered college courses and the like. Often, they are on heavyweight, "slick" paper, complete with color and black-and-white photographs and/or very artistic graphics. Often, we would look them over, drool a bit at tours and vacations beyond our reach, and throw them into "File 13."

Then one teacher came up with an idea that has proven extremely valuable in our classrooms and handled the barrage of advertising brochures that cluttered our desks.

Naturally, if this teacher wanted whatever was being advertised, he used the brochure. Otherwise, he gave them to a two-student committee he had formed. The job of these two students was to go through the brochures and clip out any interesting photographs (particularly color photos) and graphics (again, those in color were preferred). They were also advised to cut out any complete words that were particularly bold, colorful or done in an unusual graphic style.

They were also given a small stack of 6×9-inch manila clasp envelopes. On the upper left-hand corner of the face of these envelopes, they printed words that might classify the contents, such as "landscapes," "the sea," "desert" and such. **Figure 6-2** will give you a rough idea of some of the classifications and how they were written.

The two students then sorted the photos and graphics they had clipped and placed them in the appropriate envelopes. The envelopes (in this teacher's case) were kept handy on the classroom bookshelf.

Do we have to tell you how they were used? These envelopes became a first source and treasure chest for the makers of posters, book reports, term papers, bulletin boards, research papers, maps and any other school or class project that needed illustration. In the end, there were 22 envelopes, and they were being used almost every day of the school week. The two "brochure clippers" enjoyed their task, and the students and teacher enjoyed the convenience of a ready source.

That's a great deal more efficient than tossing them into the nearest refuse can.

PASSING OUT FLYERS AND BROCHURES

In the previous discussion, we spoke about advertising brochures that came to you from outside of school. Now let's look at those that come from the school and go home to your students' parents. We are always, or so it seems at times, passing out flyers about PTA Book Fairs, Saturday Softball League or a thousand and one other activities taking place at the school. It's either that, or a request for information of some type that only the home can supply. Either way, you keep passing out those brochures and flyers to your students.

One problem attendant to this procedure is keeping track of who got what. Certainly, you can save time by having a student or students pass out the material, but how many were absent on that day? The PTA wants to make certain that every home got one of their flyers, and central administration wants to make sure that all parents know about those bus schedule changes.

One teacher assigns two students to pass out all brochures and flyers, but places an added responsibility on them. They are also given the sheet in **Figure 6-3**. The class list is cut from a copy and pasted along the left-hand margin. When it comes time to pass out a flyer, the title of it is placed at the top of the particular column with its distribution date. The student aides then pass out the material, placing an X or a checkmark in the place after each name. These sheets are returned to the teacher, who keeps them until needed again or until some question about the distribution arises.

This has proven to be a quick, easy and efficient way of passing out flyers and brochures and keeping track of their dissemination. This would work well from the upper elementary grades right on through high school.

EVALUATING MATERIALS FOR FUTURE USE/PURCHASE

During your school career, it may happen that you will receive a sample of something new and be asked, as an administrative assignment, to evaluate the item for future use and/or purchase. The item may be a new piece of equipment, a learning device or, most likely, a textbook. Even if there is no money in the budget for it at this time, long-range plans may require your evaluation right now.

It will save a great deal of time if you have objective criteria on which to hang the evaluation as well as a way of storing that criteria and your report for future (and sometimes far future) reference.

Figure 6-4 shows just such a criteria sheet. This one is for a textbook to be used in a curriculum for a specific school, and you will, of course, use your own questions to suit your school and your classes.

A sheet such as this gives you direction in your evaluation. When complete, it provides a firm basis for discussion, and it is certainly easily stored in a file for future reference.

You might also want to consider making up criteria sheets for several items and entering them in the departmental or school computer. In this way, every teacher in the department or school would have equal access to them should the need arise. It might take a little longer now, but everyone in the school would benefit from it in the future.

WORKING WITH THE CLASSROOM BUDGET

Sometime during the school year, most teachers are going to be asked to prepare a classroom budget for the following year. This can take many forms, with perhaps the most common being the system in which you are assigned an arbitrary and purely symbolic amount of money, let's say $150. You are then given a list of supplies with prices, from which you order what you need for the following year up to that amount. This is turned in to department chairpersons who tally the orders, and these are sent to the school administrator who makes up the budget order for the entire school. Procedures may vary, of course, but this is essentially what happens.

Here are three hints from teachers about handling and working effectively with the classroom budget.

First, keep a record of what you order. You could make a copy of the various pages, but it's just as easy to use the sheet in **Figure 6-5**. This is an extremely simple form that may be made out *as you prepare the main form*. When you are finished preparing your budget form, your copy is also ready to be filed, and on that copy everything is together on one or two pages. You don't have to go hunting for it.

Next, make certain you file it in a place where it can be found *next year*. One teacher suggests that you start a special file just for these budget copies and flag it with a red or yellow coding dot. Next year, should there be a discrepancy in the supplies you receive, you will want to be able to find this copy in a hurry.

Finally, if there is an item that you and several other teachers want that would take up most of your budget for the item alone, get together and agree to have one teacher order the item and then spread that teacher's other supply needs among the orders of the others involved. This is particularly effective when allocations are cut and you need big figure items like large paper cutters and high priced art supplies. Just make certain a list is kept of what supplies were ordered through the other teachers for the one who sacrificed to get the big item.

You are still going to have to spend time preparing that budget, but these tips can help you get what you need for your class while making certain that you truly receive all the supplies you ordered.

MEETING WITH SALES REPRESENTATIVES

If part of your administrative duty is to meet with a sales representative, whether that person represents a textbook or science equipment company or whatever, the meeting will be a great deal easier and quicker if you can utilize the time spent in the meeting to get the information or clear up the points *you* need to know.

That sales representative is anxious to *sell* you the product, so he or she is going to stress *only* the positive points and make it sound like the greatest thing since the printing press. If you step into that and try to conduct that meeting off the top of your head, it is all but guaranteed that you will miss something.

A truly great help in this situation is to prepare a checklist as in **Figure 6-6**. With this checklist in hand, you can guide the meeting swiftly to those facts that you want to or need to know. You can also keep the meeting on track as long as you stick to the "script" that *you* have prepared. Moreover, since you can check off each item as you come to it, you can be certain that all you need is covered. The same sheet then acts as the basis for any report you may have to provide.

Naturally, you should feel free to adapt this sheet to your particular needs, and place on it whatever you need to know within your content area. This is your guide for that meeting with a sales representative, and no one knows your needs or those of your students better than you do.

REPORTING AN INCIDENT TO ADMINISTRATION

During a nonteaching, administrative assignment, something may happen that goes beyond your power to handle immediately. The child who throws something and injures another child in the cafeteria or the student you discover in a lavatory with illicit drugs is a case for the administrator of your building to handle. It is something that you must report.

Every school we know of has a process for doing this. Most require you to fill out a referral sheet. This is usually sufficient when the case is handled, and most incidents stop there. If the infraction was of a particularly serious nature (a child injured, drugs seized), however, the chances are that you will be required to recount the incident in far greater detail, particularly if the student denies it or there are legal ramifications.

Toward that end, you will find the form in **Figure 6-7** very useful. We suggest that you first go through regular school procedure immediately to handle the student and get him or her out of the situation. Then make out this far more detailed form and hand it in to the school administration sometime before the end of the school day.

When you make this out, the incident will still be fresh in your mind. The form allows you to record what happened from all viewpoints as well.

Keep a copy of this for your files. Not only will it serve as a reminder for you and as a guide for the administrator in charge, but it could even stand as evidence of the extent of your involvement if there are more serious consequences to the incident.

Later in this section, we'll talk about keeping track of day-to-day problems, and undoubtedly you will not have to utilize this special form every time you have to send a student to the office for disciplinary reasons. But for those few truly serious events in which you may be involved, it's nice to have handy.

PREPARING LESSON PLANS

We could spend paragraph upon paragraph speaking about the value of good lesson plans. Teachers understand the necessity of them, and schools everywhere require that teachers keep daily lesson plans. It is something that would be done by most educators even if it were not required.

Certainly, we would not presume to offer instruction in how to prepare a lesson plan. But it has been our experience, and that of many to whom we have spoken, that there are effective methods of cutting down the time needed to prepare lesson plans on a daily or weekly basis. Let us share one with you.

The form in **Figure 6-8** was developed by a group of teachers who were not satisfied with the plain block of space provided in most planbooks. There is no steadfast rule that your plans *must* be kept in a planbook anyhow, and many teachers prefer loose sheets because they may be more easily and quickly sorted and filed for future reference.

This form provides such adaptability. Notice that the information at the top indicates whether the plans are for a class or *classes*; so there is no need for writing "Same as Period 3" over and over if you have several classes on the same material. The textbook may be typed in when you make up this form the first time, and subsequent copies will have it already there. The sheet covers the standard five-day week, includes objectives and has a space to indicate homework.

Once you fill it out, the sheet can be copied and handed in to your supervisor or the person who checks lesson plans in your school, and you still have this to use, even if lesson plans are late getting back from administration. It tucks neatly into the corner of a desk blotter for easy and quick reference, and it can be written on and amended with ease.

The teachers who have used it like its simplicity, and we think you will also.

KEEPING AN EMERGENCY PLAN

An *emergency plan* is a plan to be used with your classes in an "emergency" when you cannot take the time to prepare something for your classes to do. There have been times when we were feeling ill, knew we would not be coming in the next day and prepared plans that were phoned in to a colleague. (See the next discussion on plans for substitute teachers.) There have also been times when we have become "suddenly ill" in school, or a tooth has needed immediate dental attention or a family matter needed "right-now" handling. At those times, there is no chance to sit down and write up plans. That's when you truly need the "emergency" plan.

From our own experience and that of a number of teachers we asked, the best emergency plan is for something that will keep the class busy and quiet and is almost self-explanatory. The best type of plan to accomplish that goal is one or two prepared worksheets, with the instructions incorporated into the worksheet itself. At the beginning of the school year, run these off in sufficient quantities for all your classes.

On top of these, place the cover sheet found in **Figure 6-9**. This sheet (filled out, of course) gives all the information that a hall duty teacher or someone else called in on an emergency basis might need to know for handling the class and the materials on the "spur of the moment."

Place all of this into *one* package where it will easily be found. Tell a colleague or friend where it is. (See the following discussion.)

We hope that you will never have an emergency that takes you out of school. If it should happen, however, this simple procedure will help to keep order in your classroom and enable students to learn in your absence.

LEAVING PLANS FOR THE SUBSTITUTE TEACHER

The plans you make up are useless unless they get into the hands of your substitute teacher. In one situation, near bedlam reigned for virtually an entire day because the plans weren't found until the last period under the absent teacher's desk blotter.

Let's look at three suggestions from experienced teachers that will prevent such an incident.

First, make certain that at least two other teachers know where they are and will take responsibility for telling your substitute. This simple expedient saves so much turmoil, that it is amazing that it is not a required action in all schools.

Second, consider going in with two or more teachers and establishing a central place where *all of you* leave your lesson plans *all the time*. Check in with each other every morning, and if one of you is missing, give plans to the substitute and take care of all points of school "business" for the missing colleague. If you have formed a particular friendship with two or three other teachers in a school, this would be a fine way to help each other, your school and your students.

Finally, make a firm arrangement with a "buddy." This is a person or colleague, whom you will personally call if you are going to be out. At that time, you will dictate to this person your specific lesson plans or instructions or where certain materials are located. This person takes it all down and agrees to give the message to your substitute. Of course, it is understood that you will return the service whenever your "buddy" needs it.

Here are three quick suggestions to ensure that your lesson plans get into the hands of your substitute. They are fast, easily accomplished, and keep your classes running smoothly.

SUPERVISING THE HALLS

Some schools call them "Nonteaching Duties," while other places call them "Administrative Assignments." Whatever the terminology, these are duties of a supervisory capacity that a teacher is assigned outside the classroom. It may be watching over the lunch room, serving in the library or main office, or, as we will concentrate on here, supervising the halls of the school as classes are in session.

Our school calls it "Hall Duty," and here are a few hints about this assignment from teachers who have had some experience in the area.

Sit down. Use a student desk (if you can fit), or use a desk for a surface to work on and a folding chair to sit in.

Ask the assigning administrator if your hall duty can be on the same floor as your classroom (for easy access to your papers, etc.) or switch locations with another teacher if possible.

This is a "quiet" duty most of the time. Use it to correct papers or work on classroom planning and activities.

At least twice during your duty, walk the assigned area. It's good exercise, and you never know what you might find.

Check the lavatories at least twice.

Vary the time when you walk and check each day. Don't get into a routine where students know your checking "schedule."

Keep a separate sheet of paper, a "Hall Duty Log," and record in it the day and time of *any* unusual activity. (See Figure 6-10.)

Check student passes. Send students with no passes back to their teachers for them.

These suggestions can save you a great deal of time and help you turn an otherwise uneventful assignment into one that allows you to get some of your work done while providing security for the students and the school.

SUPERVISION DURING ADMINISTRATIVE ASSIGNMENTS

The majority of the time most teachers spend on administrative assignments is without incident, and the incidents that do occur are minor. Every so often an incident will occur during your duty that will tax your skills of supervision, but these are the exception rather than the rule.

Earlier in this section, we referred you to Figure 6-7 to use when you had to report one of these serious infractions. Many teachers also have found a need for keeping a record of *anything* out of the ordinary that happens during an administrative assignment.

Perhaps a child is out of class without a pass from the teacher. A student visits the lavatory three times in the same period. A pupil runs down the hallway in an agitated manner. In most cases, these incidents mean little or nothing. But should any of them turn into a more complicated problem (possibly involving guidance, the school administration, the home or other outside authorities), there is certainly the possibility that you will be further involved and even asked to remember facts about the incident even though it may have occurred some time ago. This can be troublesome.

Consequently, we suggest you keep a record of *any* unusual incident that happens during your administrative assignment. The sheet in **Figure 6-10** is an example of something you might tuck into the back of your marking book and carry around until such time as an unusual or notable incident occurs during your administrative assignment. Using the very simple guidelines on this sheet, you will have sufficient information to spur your memory should the incident have to be recalled in detail at some later time.

APPLYING SCHOOL RULES OUTSIDE THE CLASSROOM

We are all diligent in enforcing the rules of the school as well as our own rules within our classrooms. Certainly, we realize that if anything is going to be accomplished, it is best done in a place where order reigns.

There are times, however, when we are not in our classrooms, and we witness things happening that go against school rules. When this happens, when the students involved are not under our direct supervision, or when it would be easier and less time-consuming to just walk away, what do we do? We all recognize the strong temptation to turn away and pretend that we saw nothing. Why put in time and effort on something that does not even involve one of our kids?

An older and more experienced teacher once told us that the surest time-saver is to "never look the other way." Whether we like it or not, teachers get a "reputation" with students. Some teachers are considered "soft" or "a pushover," while others are "strict," "firm and fair," and students know that "you can't put anything over on her." These reputations help greatly in achieving and maintaining a teacher's discipline throughout the school year.

You build that reputation one step at a time, and you make it a positive and no-nonsense reputation by *always* applying and enforcing school rules *wherever you are*. Whether you use Figure 6-10 or jot down a name on a notecard to be dealt with later, students will know that you apply the school rules all the time, and you will have gained a reputation that will help you in your daily classroom routine.

As that teacher said, the surest time-saver is to "never look the other way!"

TEACHER CHECKLIST OF ADMINISTRATIVE DUTIES

Most teachers serve administrative duties year after year without incidents of any kind beyond the ordinary that might be expected in a school. Other teachers, however, have found it necessary to document that they fulfilled their administrative duties or to identify the precise number of times and dates when they performed a special assignment, such as covering a class or someone else's duty.

An incident happened in the hallway two weeks ago on Friday, and administration is asking if you were on your assigned hall duty to notice and deal with it at that time. The School Board has a policy about the number of times a teacher may be asked to cover another teacher's class or duty within a specified time period, and you are being questioned as to the number of times you performed that function. This information can be a real headache to supply if you are not prepared to do so.

A checklist of your administrative duties as in **Figure 6-11** can help you in that situation. After you have filled in the required information, this sheet details your administrative duties for a month at a time. All you do is check off the appropriate space as you complete each duty. There is also space available to indicate "special administrative assignments," such as classes covered or special supervisory assignments.

Combine this with Figures 6-7 and 6-10, and you will have all the information that you will need to answer any question that guidance, the administration or anyone else could want to ask you about your administrative duties.

This has to be used only once to prove its value. Start a new sheet for each month and keep the filled-out ones on file for at least a year. It will be comforting to know that the information is there should any question arise.

TO BE ANSWERED
at the October 10th Departmental Meeting

1. Will you have to change your plans for the month of November?

2. How will the new grading system affect YOU for this first marking period?

3. Will the new grading system mean extra work for you?

4. How will you handle the computer cards?

5. When, if ever, are we going to get the new textbooks we talked about all last year?

6. While we're at it, where are the supplies that were missing back in September?

7. What will the change in insurance carriers mean to me and my family?

To find out, bring this sheet with you to the meeting, Room #201, 3:00p.m. sharp!

**Lynn Villa,
Dept. Chair.**

Figure 6-1
Questions-to-Be-Answered Sheet

✂ To Be Clipped ✂

The Sea	Landscapes	Food
Sea Storms	The Desert	Vegetables
Calm Sea	Mountains	Meats
Waves on Rocks	Snow Scenes	Breads
Waves on Sand	Winter Sports	Desserts
Rivers	City Life	Italian Food
Lakes	City Life at Night	Chinese Food
Water Sports	City Shops	Mexican Food
Men and Women	Other Countries	Cooking
Children	Airplanes (Air Lines)	Table Settings
Doctors/Nurses	Airplanes (Military)	Bar-B-Que
Teachers	Trucks	Restaurants
Lawyers	Cars (Regular)	Groceries
Police	Cars (Fast)	Shopping

Any Words That Are Over One Inch High and/or Unusual

Figure 6-2
Advertising Brochure Management Form

Item Out: _____

Date Out:_____ Date Due Back:_____

Student	Out	Returned
_____	( )	( )
_____	( )	( )
_____	( )	( )
_____	( )	( )
_____	( )	( )
_____	( )	( )
_____	( )	( )
_____	( )	( )
_____	( )	( )
_____	( )	( )
_____	( )	( )
_____	( )	( )
_____	( )	( )
_____	( )	( )
_____	( )	( )

Figure 6-3
Flyer Distribution Checklist

Item evaluated: _____

Title/Author: _____

Publisher:_____

Contact person: _____

Address: _____

Telephone: _____ Fax: _____

Evaluator: _____

First impression of book: _____

_____

_____

Age appropriate: _____

Estimated life of book: _____

Comments on binding: _____

Illustrations: _____

Quality of paper: _____

Ease of repair: _____

Scope of content: _____

_____

_____

How is this better/worse than present textbook: _____

_____

_____

Recommendations: _____

_____

_____

_____

Signature of evaluator: _____

Date: _____

Figure 6-4
Textbook Evaluation Criteria

Page	Item #	Item	Quant.	Price	Total

Teacher: _____ Date: _____

Classroom Budget for the School Year _____ - _____

Amount Allocated: _____ Amount Used: _____

Page _____ of _____

Figure 6-5
Budget Order Record Form

Teacher:_____ Date:_____

Sales Rep. & Co.:_____

Product:_____

1. ( ) What advantage(es) over what we have now?

2. ( ) Product tested/piloted?

3. ( ) Durability (life span) of product?

4. ( ) Reproducibles and transparencies available?

5. ( ) Workbook and worksheets available?

6. ( ) Comprehensiveness of Teacher's Edition?

7. ( ) Extent of teacher training involved?

8. ( ) Will company conduct workshop(s)?

9. ( ) What is the unit price?

10. ( ) Discounts available for quantity?

Figure 6-6
Sales Meeting Checklist

Teacher: _____ Date: _____

INCIDENT REPORT

Location of incident: _____

Time of occurrence: Date: _____ Time of day: _____
Student(s) involved: _____

Adult(s) involved: _____

If injury, to whom and to what extent: _____

Witness(es) to incident: _____

Action taken by reporting teacher at time of incident: _____

Description of incident: _____

_____

_____

_____

_____

_____

_____

Comments: _____

_____

_____

_____

Figure 6-7
Student Incident Report

	HOMEWORK:
Teacher: _____ Grade: _____ Lesson Plans for Class(es) [Period(s)]: _____ For the Time Period From _____ to _____ Text(s): _____ Other Materials: ____	

MONDAY _____
  Objective(s):
 	
  Method(s):
	HOMEWORK:

TUESDAY _____
  Objective(s):
 	
  Method(s):
	HOMEWORK:

WEDNESDAY _____
  Objective(s):
 	
  Method(s):
	HOMEWORK:

THURSDAY _____
  Objective(s):
 	
  Method(s):
	HOMEWORK:

FRIDAY _____
  Objective(s):
 	
  Method(s):
	HOMEWORK:

Of Special Note:	

Figure 6-8
Weekly Lesson Plan Form

EMERGENCY PLANS

Teacher: _____

Plans for which class(es) or period(s): _____
_____

Location of seating charts and materials: _____
_____
_____

Instructions: _____
_____
_____
_____
_____
_____
_____
_____

Special comments: _____
_____
_____
_____
_____
_____
_____
_____
_____

Figure 6-9
Emergency Plans Worksheet

| Teacher: _____ |
| Administrative assignment: _____ |
| Location: _____ |

Date & Time	What Happened?	Who Was Involved?

Figure 6-10
Administrative Assignment Incident Form

| Teacher: _____ School year: _____ |
| Administrative assignment: _____ |
| Location: _____ |
| For the month of _____ ,19 _____ |

DATE:	Covered	Not Covered	DATE:	Covered	Not Covered
_____	( )	( )	_____	( )	( )
_____	( )	( )	_____	( )	( )
_____	( )	( )	_____	( )	( )
_____	( )	( )	_____	( )	( )
_____	( )	( )	_____	( )	( )
_____	( )	( )	_____	( )	( )
_____	( )	( )	_____	( )	( )
_____	( )	( )	_____	( )	( )
_____	( )	( )	_____	( )	( )
_____	( )	( )	_____	( )	( )
_____	( )	( )	_____	( )	( )
_____	( )	( )	_____	( )	( )
_____	( )	( )	_____	( )	( )
_____	( )	( )	_____	( )	( )
_____	( )	( )	_____	( )	( )

SPECIAL ADMINISTRATIVE ASSIGNMENTS: _____
_____
_____
_____

Figure 6-11
Administrative Duties Checklist

LARGE AND SMALL GROUP MANAGEMENT

As teachers, we work with groups of students a great deal of the time. From supervising students on the playground, at lunch or on the major class trip, to the work that we do with groups within our individual classrooms, groups of children are a part of every teacher's life. Let's look at several suggestions for saving time and trouble in our efforts with large and small group management.

MONITORING STUDENTS ON THE PLAYGROUND

Previously, we detailed ways in which several teachers assigned to the same duty might increase the effectiveness of their supervision in an area such as the school playground. Here, however, we are talking about *one* teacher who must supervise a group or class within the same area. This might occur when teachers take their class out for recess or just "for a break," or it might be for a science-related activity searching for insect life or leaf gathering. Whatever the case, there is a full class on the field—and one teacher.

An elementary teacher we know suggests that this is not an activity for teachers to do on their own. You need help in these cases, and you find it in your class. The secret of handling one large group is to make certain that it is broken up into several smaller groups, each with someone in charge.

Well in advance of the first "outing," you would prepare some sort of list as that in **Figure 7-1**. You will notice a space for Group Leader, followed by slots for the names of group members. Since you know your class best, you will know which students to place in each group, including one that you would personally supervise.

Once out on the field, all "common" problems are handled by the group leaders who would be responsible for such things as seeing to it that reports, equipment and the like are collected and returned to you. Of course, should any problems arise, they would seek your assistance immediately, and you would be close enough to handle any emergency.

This may not be the solution to every playground or field problem, but it is much easier to deal with four or five students than with 25 or 30, and that's what the Group Leader approach provides. Preparing your list in advance, with some thought to accurate student placement and familiarizing your class with it, should make the experience of taking a class into the open field a good deal easier.

MONITORING STUDENTS AT LUNCH

Of course, we can't speak for you, but around our school, the all-time *least* favorite administrative assignment is *lunch duty*. Now, if you have lunchroom aides in your school, you may not need to read any further, but if you are one of the many who must walk the floors of the cafeteria or lunchroom while a host of children consume their lunches, then we offer several suggestions from veterans that will help you better survive the experience.

Decide on how many boys and girls may be out of the cafeteria at one time for lavatory use. Then make that number of passes out of wood or masonite or some other durable material. *One* teacher is to be in charge of these, and you establish the rule that there is *one* student out on a pass at any time. Another student cannot leave until the pass is returned.

Next, assign each teacher a section of the area. Most likely, this will be a specific number of tables. That teacher is responsible for *that area only*, with the understanding, of course, that common sense will prevail should help be needed in another section.

Finally, you might want to use a Table Map as in **Figure 7-2**. Of course, your Table Map would represent *your* lunchroom. It is made *once* and copied as needed from then on. On it, you could list the teachers and areas for which they are responsible, the names of teacher or student monitors assigned to each table, the names of students who may have been assigned to a table, patterns of movement for entry or dismissal and a host of other uses that will certainly occur to you as the school year goes on.

It would also be wise for one teacher to be assigned as a historian to record any unusual events and/or student discipline problems, as we suggested in the last section.

While Lunch Duty may never become pleasant, it can be survivable and made to run smoothly when all cooperate for the common good.

MOVING STUDENTS THROUGH THE HALLS

Sooner or later, we are all faced with the necessity of guiding our class through the hallways of the school to a specific location. It might be for an assembly, vision or hearing checks, or a library visit, but you have to get the class out of the room, through the hallways, possibly down or up flights of stairs and to the destination—all without losing a student or making such a din that education comes to a standstill in the rest of the school.

While such an undertaking hardly requires something akin to the plans for the Normandy Invasion, you will find that it goes a great deal easier, considerably quicker, and with far less headaches, if you do advance planning.

Typical of that planning might be the sheet in **Figure 7-3**. Determine the exact route your class will take to get from your classroom to your destination. Along that route, note strategically important points to your passage: any corner that must be turned, the tops and bottoms of stairs, doorways (particularly "swinging" doorways) that must be held open and passed through. Indicate these as checkpoints along your route.

Assign a responsible student from the class to each of the checkpoints. As the class leaves the room, the student assigned to the first checkpoint goes on ahead to that point. As the last of the class passes that checkpoint, the student falls in at the rear. Meanwhile, the student assigned to the next checkpoint goes on ahead and stands at his or her post. So it proceeds until the class has reached its destination.

What do these students do? Basically, they just stand there. If there is any trouble or if there are stragglers, they report it to you. They are to be "exhorters," urging the other students to keep up, keep quiet and keep on the right path. Actually, their very presence *does* keep the class on task, keeps them from creating too much noise and generally makes the passage an uneventful one.

Try this once, and you will be using it for those occasions when you and your class must venture out into the wide world of your school's hallways.

ESTABLISHING SMALL GROUPS FOR LEARNING (I)

It is not our purpose here or in the next discussion to touch on Cooperative Learning, except to say that it is something well worth any educator's time to investigate. Rather, we are going to look at some methods that teachers have used to establish small groups of students for group work within the classroom.

We observed a classroom once where all the "bright" children had been grouped together, and all the "slow learners" shared a group. Bedlam reigned! The "slows" did everything but work, and they fought constantly; the "brights" got nothing done either—they were busy battling to see who would control the group.

It would have been better for everyone, particularly the children, if names written on slips of paper had been drawn from a paper bag. This approach promotes eclectic and random grouping.

If you have a specific project in mind, and you are forming the groups for the successful completion of that project, both in terms of product and process, then you might want to use the form in **Figure 7-4**. Naturally, you would adapt this form to your specific requirements, but its general use remains the same.

Head a list with a "type" that the project will need. Such words as *artist, writer, researcher* come to mind, but you select those that your project requires. Under each heading, place the names of students in your class who are particularly good in that area. This may take a bit of sound reflection, but stick to it until everyone is allocated a position on the list.

Now, as you form a group, pick one student from each classification needed for the group's proper functioning. Try also to have a mix of academic abilities in each group, including a top student and one who needs more help in each group. The result should be a group with sufficient skills to produce the product and with sufficient interaction to enhance the process as well.

ESTABLISHING SMALL GROUPS FOR LEARNING (II)

What about allowing students to select their own group members? Is that merely inviting trouble? Won't kids select their friends and then spend most of the time "fooling around"? Isn't it just a waste of time?

The answer to these questions is a definite yes, *unless*, that is, the choice is properly guided.

You can give your students the practice in making wise choices while ensuring that the groups they select will work rather than play if you take a little time to establish guidelines for their free choices. It will save a great deal of time and trouble later on.

Figure 7-5 is a criteria sheet established by one teacher for her students' selection of groups in which to work. This sheet is representative of one teacher and must be adapted to *your* particular needs.

With this criteria sheet, you are ready to allow your students to select their own groups. The teacher who developed this particular sheet would explain it to her class and have each student make up a sheet of paper on which he or she listed his or her first choices according to the criteria given. Then, she allowed them five minutes to interact with each other and literally "negotiate" the composition of the groups. Finally, she established a set time a few minutes hence when all final group lists had to be turned in.

According to this teacher, she has never had a problem with the class failing to meet the deadline.

GETTING MATERIALS TO GROUPS

Once you have established your groups and given them the directions and parameters they need, you must address certain logistical matters. One such matter involves getting the needed materials to each group to successfully complete the project.

Toward that end, let us share with you a method that ensures that every group has everything they need and, at the same time, gives the group practice in planning skills and cooperating for success.

For this, we will use the form in **Figure 7-6**. Pass out one of these to each group, who will, in turn, fill it out after thought and discussion among themselves. Set a time limit for the completion of the form. You might also strongly suggest that the group choose *one* person to act as liaison between the teacher and the group.

Now, with form in hand, the person in charge comes to you, shows you the sheet with the material requirements of the group, and either takes or is given what the group has determined it needs to succeed. These materials are checked off as they are received.

The great advantage to this method is that you, the teacher, have one person to deal with from each group and that person, not you, is responsible for garnering and then distributing materials to the group. That person must make certain that everyone in the group has the materials needed to complete the project. Not only does this provide the students with valuable experience in planning ahead, cooperative learning and working together for a common goal, but, in most cases we have observed, it frees the teachers to be the educational innovator and leader that group work requires rather than a poor imitation of an Army Supply Sergeant.

COLLECTING MATERIALS FROM GROUPS

You can successfully use the same process detailed in the previous discussion to retrieve used materials or equipment from groups.

Few things are more frustrating than to lend out an article and not have it returned. Often the teacher is very busy when the request for something (let's say scissors) is made. Under that pressure, the article may be given out and then forgotten as the class progresses and there is more and more for the teacher to do. It may be only later, when *you* need to get that article, that you recall the scissors were lent and apparently not returned.

You can use the same sheet in **Figure 7-6** to effectively deal with that problem. If you recall, the advantage

of using that sheet is that you now deal with only one person from the group, and that person must "sign out" all materials needed by the group for the project. You can solve the problem of getting materials *back* from the group by merely reversing the process. *Nothing* is given out to the group *except* through this one representative of the group. In like manner, that *one* representative is responsible for returning all borrowed, nonconsumable materials (like scissors). If you use the sheet and require the person to sign out on all materials, also require the representative to sign in all materials returned.

You now have a record of what went out, to whom it went and when it was returned. You are dealing with four or five people rather than 25 or 30 individuals. Anything missing is clearly evident and may be handled on the spot, and, since the group representatives know they will be held responsible, materials are usually returned promptly.

That's a real plus in any group situation.

DEALING WITH GROUP DISTRACTIONS

Has it ever happened that you have assigned a group a project and they have failed to complete it or completed it in an unsatisfactory manner? When this happened, did the excuses start flowing? We didn't have enough time. We couldn't find what we needed. Denny wouldn't stop fooling around. And so it goes. In short, they were full of reasons that distracted them from the accomplishment of their goal and why they couldn't complete what they set out to do.

Deal effectively with group distractions by eliminating them *before* they become distractions. While this may be obvious, is it not easier said than done?

Take a look at **Figure 7-7**. One teacher gives this to each group once he has explained the necessity of completing the project. He gives students time to think about it and discuss it within the group before they fill it out together. Allot some time for this purpose.

How can these completed papers be used? They could be a spur to group discussions of ways to overcome common problems. If the distractions mentioned are temporal ones, such as a lack of materials or time, perhaps changes can be made to allow the group to eliminate the problem. If the distractions are personal, such as personality conflicts, perhaps the group structure needs to be reevaluated. If the distractions listed by the group are absolutely frivolous, such as not wanting to do this "dumb thing," then the teacher must stress the importance of cooperation.

Whatever the approach, handling the possible distractions *before* they occur takes away virtually all excuses for not completing the project. It also gives students the opportunity to grow in the appreciation of their responsibility in the completion of the work.

In any case, it certainly saves you time as all distractions that could lead to group confusion or even group "shutdown" are not only anticipated but dealt with effectively.

THE "PICKED-ON" GROUP MEMBER

Some students, for a variety of reasons, become the focus of other students' aggression and may be "picked on" by others. This is bad enough when it happens in the class as a whole, but when it happens in a group, it can mean that the entire group will be in trouble and little or nothing will get done. Nor does it bode well for the learning experience of the picked-on group member.

Let us share two methods for dealing with this situation within a group setting.

First, let's examine the possibility that the picked-on student may share at least some of the responsibility for the aggression mounted against himself or herself. Students, for instance, who constantly mock others, deride their work or actions, or tease or taunt may find themselves in a position where there is decided hostility expressed by a student who has "had it" with taunts and mockery. In this case, a very effective method of handling it is to make it clear that if there is an incident, there will be a punishment forthcoming—for both parties. If the picked-on student is found to be at fault, then the aggressor and the person who is the object of the aggression will receive the same punishment. This really works and cuts down dramatically on such incidents.

If, however, the picked-on student has done nothing to occasion the incidents, then you must try other approaches. One teacher explained that if she has a child in a group who has truly, and through no fault of his or her own, become the object of attack, she will try to manufacture some situation where the group, and particularly the other members of the group, must rely on the picked-on child. Then, she will pull some strings and see to it that the child succeeds. For instance, she might tell the group that one person *must* explain exactly what the group is doing, and that person is Alison (the picked-on). Then, after a short time for Alison to prepare, she will listen to her, praise her presentation, and explain to the group that Alison has really helped them and how she really understands them now.

If either approach works in your situation, you will have eliminated a possible time-consuming stumbling block.

AVOIDING GROUP DOMINATION

We all realize that one of the reasons we give group work is to teach kids how to work together. That means everyone does his or her job and works in unison to accomplish the common, group-set goal. As we all know only too well, it doesn't always work that way.

One of the obstacles that keeps group members from learning by participating occurs when the group is "taken over" by one student. Perhaps *dominated* would be a better word. Usually, this is a very strong student who immediately takes over and begins directing—telling the other children in the group what to do. Of course, he or she has not been elected to this position but has assumed it and the other group members have acquiesced.

A physical education teacher suggests that when this happens, you use the strength of the dominating individual to clear up the problem.

Suppose you become aware that one group is really being dominated by Fred. He won't allow others to get in a word. He already has everything planned out his way, and the others just sit, waiting to be told what to do.

Take Fred aside and tell him that you are concerned about the group he is in. Tell him that you have noticed that most of the students in the group are not participating as they should. Now tell Fred that you noticed his leadership abilities, and because of that, you have a special task for him. Fred is to see to it that from now on, everyone in the group participates or talks or works *equally*. This is now Fred's job, and he will be held responsible for it. You might even have him report to you on a set basis to give progress reports, although you will certainly be in a position to observe progress firsthand.

In short, you have used the strength that brought the person to dominance in the first place to ensure that the dominance gradually decreases as others begin to take a greater and greater part in the group and in the process.

GIVING EVERYONE A CHANCE

Sometimes you place students into certain groups to give them expertise at various functions within the group. Let us say, for example, that you have six microscopes for the entire class. You divide the class into six groups, each with a project that requires microscope work. In this way, or so it would seem, each student gains experience working with the microscope. What a great idea.

It doesn't always work that way. One or two students in the group may become highly enamored of the microscope and hog the instrument to themselves, allowing others a half-second peek every now and then. That's not a great learning experience for those who are excluded from the main action.

In this case, our task is to make certain that everyone has a chance, and one way to do this is to see to it that no one in the group is doing anything in the group for longer than a day.

You can adapt the list in **Figure 7-8** for such a project to whatever project you have assigned. The list details all the "jobs" in the group. Note that there are as many jobs as there are people to fill them. Give this list to the group to be made out and handed in to you at the end of each day, with the understanding that this is the job assignment for the *next* school day. The only criterion given to the group is that no one person in the group can hold a job a second time until *everyone* has had a chance to hold it at least once. In other words, *every* child gets to use the microscope.

Obviously, you will not need to use this method with every group you form, but for those occasions where you want to ensure that every student has an equal opportunity with every job in the group, this method is not only quick, but works well in solving this problem.

THE CLASS TRIP (I)

Let's talk about a situation involving large group management that is surely faced by every teacher sooner or later—the class trip.

A class trip that involves transporting a large student group from the school to a destination, supervising them at the destination, and transporting them back to the school can contain enough variables to test the strength and moral fiber of the strongest of teachers. It is not, however, an impossible task and can run a great deal smoother if we take to heart the suggestions of some educators with a great deal of experience in this area.

The first time- and effort-saving suggestion is to find out all the information you need to know *before* you announce the trip. Sit down with a sheet of paper and list *everything* you will need to know—availability of buses, time of presentation at destination, special procedures and the like. To determine the cost per student, take *all* expenses (total bus cost, fees at destination, tips for bus drivers) and divide by the number of *students* going. Round off this figure to the next highest dollar. This is student cost.

Now, investigate *all* (and we do mean *all*) your school's policies and procedures relative to a field trip. This might include the filing of a statement of educational value, making out an impact study, listing provisions for students not going, provisions to be made for those with medical problems and the like. *Then and only then* are you ready to announce the trip.

Set a time for money and permission slips to be in. Don't take permission slips without money or money without permission slips, and keep a record of everything. With those kids who are late or "forgot," try taking them down to the office and standing behind them as they call home. That gets it in the next day.

All this may seem like a lot of work, but for the headaches that *don't* occur and the time *not* wasted having to explain again and again, it truly qualifies as time- and effort-saving activity.

THE CLASS TRIP (II)

Eventually, the day of the class trip will arrive. Your first problem involves the transportation of your students from the school to the destination. The same problem applies *after* the day's activities, when the students must be transported back to the school.

In the next discussion, we'll talk about tips for handling your group at the destination, but for now, let's look at some suggestions for saving time and trouble when handling groups as they are being transported to and from the trip destination.

First, publish a list of *only* those students going, and further break it down to only those going on a particular bus. Then, make a checkoff list for several *key points* in the transportation process. Certainly, every time a bus is boarded, even if it is to be taken around the block, is a key point. These are times to check a student's presence on the bus. **Figure 7-9** is an example of such a list, but yours will be personalized to your particular agenda.

You can use this list in a number of ways. A teacher who knows all the children going on the trip may stand at the bus door and check off names as they enter. Students, under supervision, may be required to initial or sign in their presence (this takes longer, but is absolute verification). Or the list may be "called" by the supervisor. Whatever you do, you now have a single place where the attendance of each child is verified as the bus is boarded and no possibility of the nightmare of leaving a child behind.

Distribute bus chaperones evenly along the entire length of the bus, and there will be little trouble with behavior during the trip as well.

Getting there may not be half the fun of the trip, but it can be made a good deal more pleasant and effective with the organization suggested here.

THE CLASS TRIP (III)

Now let's take a look at what we can do once the group has reached the destination. We have to get them safely through whatever there is to do and back on the bus, presumably having learned something in the process.

Depending on what type of place you are visiting, you may wish to break the larger group into several smaller groups, each with one or two chaperones in charge. If this is the case, it would be wise to make up a sheet similar to the one in **Figure 7-9** except for the small group. Take attendance every time they enter or leave an activity/area. Impress on your group that *nobody* leaves or goes on to the next phase until *everyone* is accounted for. Making group members responsible for each other should serve you well.

If your destination is of such a nature that keeping small groups together is all but impossible, you might want to try an approach using the sheet in **Figure 7-10**. Again this is a list of names in a group followed by certain locations at the destination and times of the day. Reproduce this and give it to each person in the group. Wherever they go, they must meet at the location and at the time listed. There, the teacher merely takes attendance and they are off again. Make clear, however, that the group must remain at the location until *everyone* has checked in. Again, the group will tend to police itself to see that everyone adheres to the schedule.

Whichever technique seems appropriate, you can see the built-in trouble-saving advantages. Not only do you have a "running total" throughout the day, but you also have made students aware that they must watch over each other.

CHECKLIST FOR TRIP EVALUATION

Once the class trip is over, and you have had a chance to relax and toss off the stress that such an activity produces, your mind should turn toward the recent trip. You tend to wonder about what you have just been through.

Although it is finished for this school year, there will be another and new class next year. Should this trip be considered for them? Was it worthwhile? Was it more trouble than it was worth? Were there special problems inherent in it? Were these problems difficult? Did they cause trouble? Were they easily overcome? What were the educational advantages? How did these balance out against the disadvantages?

Even if you can evaluate the trip and keep all that information in your mind, will it all be fresh next year when you want it? Could you share it with a fellow teacher who is interested in the same trip?

Figure 7-11 contains what might be termed a Field Trip Evaluation Form. While all the details are still fresh in your mind, take a few moments to fill it out. You can include as many particulars as you wish and make whatever comments you desire. When you are finished, not only will you have "vented" yourself, but you will have a tangible appraisal of the trip to store or use for future reference or share with a colleague.

Doing it now will save you considerable time and effort in planning next year, as well as give you a facility and ease of operation that will be definitely appreciated come trip time next year.

PLAYGROUND SUPERVISION

Group Leader _____

Group Leader _____

_____
_____
_____
_____

_____
_____
_____
_____

Group Leader _____

Group Leader _____

_____
_____
_____
_____

_____
_____
_____
_____

Group Leader _____

Group Leader _____

_____
_____
_____
_____

_____
_____
_____
_____

Figure 7-1
Playground Supervision Sheet

Figure 7-2
Cafeteria Table Map

FROM: Room #205   TO: Library

ROUTE	CHECK POINT MONITORS
CHECKPOINT: Classroom Door Out door, turn right	**Martin Chen**
CHECKPOINT: End of Hall Down hall to end, turn right	**Natasha Kurin**
CHECKPOINT: Doors at Top of Stairs Through doors and down stairs	**Nancy Butano** **Kevin Kallner**
CHECKPOINT: Doors at Bottom of Stairs Through doors and turn right	**Lannel Coy** **Billy Primmert**
CHECKPOINT: Guidance Office Door Continue down hallway to Guidance office, turn left	**Murita Salaveras**
CHECKPOINT: Library Door Through Library door and into Library	**Edwin Sorinski**

Figure 7-3
Hallway Planning Sheet

PROJECT: Student Movement Flowchart

ARTISTS

( ) Tommy Bates
( ) Frank Reitzel
( ) Reynaldo Giron
( ) Jean Schweitzer
( ) Ingrid Pedersen

RESEARCH

( ) Natasha Kurin
( ) Basilio Ponce
( ) Kwan Li
( ) Connie Barber
( ) Susan Pease

WRITER

( ) Susan Edwards
( ) Terry Morgan
( ) Wes Whalen
( ) Harry Hansen
( ) Jill Barnes

MODEL MAKER

( ) Gilbert Hernadian
( ) Jerry Signore
( ) Kelly MacIntyre
( ) Daniel Farwicz
( ) Stanley Danowski

ASSISTANCE (all fields)

( ) Carol Cacossa
( ) Barbara Ross
( ) Bobby Benson
( ) Aaron Schmidt
( ) Victoria Taylor

Figure 7-4
Group Formation Form

YOUR NAME: _____

In your group you must have:

( )   no more than four (4) people
( )   two (2) boys and two (2) girls
( )   no more than one (1) close friend
( )   people you feel will work well

These are the people I would like to have in my group:

ME:_____
First Choice:_____
Second Choice:_____
Third Choice:_____

Does your list reflect the criteria given above?   If not, re-think your list.

Figure 7-5
Group Selection Criteria Sheet

GROUP NUMBER: _____

NEEDED MATERIALS LIST

Group Rep: _____

Member: _____

Member: _____

Member: _____

This is what we need to successfully complete our project:

( ) _____

( ) _____

( ) _____

( ) _____

( ) _____

( ) _____

( ) _____

( ) _____

( ) _____

( ) _____

Figure 7-6
Group Material Requirements Form

GROUP NUMBER: _____   DATE: _____

Group Rep: _____
Member: _____
Member: _____
Member: _____

Think about it; discuss it; then write down five things that might KEEP YOU FROM COMPLETING THE PROJECT. Don't leave anything blank.

1.   _____
        _____

2.   _____
        _____

3.   _____
        _____

4.   _____
        _____

5.   _____
        _____

Figure 7-7
Group Distraction Evaluation Guide

GROUP NUMBER: _____

GROUP ASSIGNMENTS FOR (date): _____

Journal Keeper: _____
Specimen Handler: _____
Microscope: _____
Recorder: _____

REMINDER: This sheet must be turned in to the teacher by the end of class or jobs for the following day will be assigned by the teacher.

Figure 7-8
Job Distribution Sheet

Date: _____ **Destination:** _____

Teacher in Charge: _____ **Bus No.** _____

STUDENTS	Check Pt. 1	Check Pt. 2	Check Pt. 3
_____	[ ]	[ ]	[ ]
_____	[ ]	[ ]	[ ]
_____	[ ]	[ ]	[ ]
_____	[ ]	[ ]	[ ]
_____	[ ]	[ ]	[ ]
_____	[ ]	[ ]	[ ]
_____	[ ]	[ ]	[ ]
_____	[ ]	[ ]	[ ]
_____	[ ]	[ ]	[ ]
_____	[ ]	[ ]	[ ]
_____	[ ]	[ ]	[ ]
_____	[ ]	[ ]	[ ]
_____	[ ]	[ ]	[ ]
_____	[ ]	[ ]	[ ]
_____	[ ]	[ ]	[ ]
_____	[ ]	[ ]	[ ]
_____	[ ]	[ ]	[ ]
_____	[ ]	[ ]	[ ]
_____	[ ]	[ ]	[ ]

Figure 7-9
Group Transportation Checklist

Group number: _____   Date: _____

Teacher: _____

This group will meet at the following locations at the time given. Attendance WILL be taken.

TIME   PLACE

10:00 A.M.   The STATUE OF THE DOLPHIN located just outside
                    the Main Entrance.

12:00 NOON   LOBBY area just outside the CAFETERIA.

2:00 P.M.   BUS LOADING AREA NUMBER 3.

Please remember — the entire group will remain at the location until EVERYONE in the group has checked in. BE THERE AND BE ON TIME.

Figure 7-10
Small Group Attendance Plan

FIELD TRIP EVALUATION FORM

(This form is provided for the teacher's personal records as an aid in evaluating and planning
  future field trips.)

Date of Trip:_____
Group Taken:_____
Teachers:_____
Nature of Trip:_____
Bus Carrier:_____

HOW WOULD YOU RATE	LOW	2	3	4	5	HIGH
Bus Service_____						
Student Interest_____						
Simplicity of Arrangements_____						
Treatment at Destination_____						
Educational Value_____						

Would you take this trip again?   [   ] YES   [   ] NO

Why or why not?_____
_____
_____

Overall evaluation of trip:_____
_____
_____

Figure 7-11
Class Trip Evaluation Checklist

MANAGING CLASSROOM ROUTINE

Most classrooms that we visit are colorful, pleasant places. Perhaps one reason for this is the fact that most of our time in school is spent in one room. It is only natural that we would wish to establish a warm and happy atmosphere in which to live and function. This applies not only to the physical setup of the room, but to its day-to-day operation as well. In this section, let's take a look at some methods used to efficiently handle the daily functioning of that place we know so well—the classroom.

THOSE OPENING EXERCISES

In our school, the day has a very definite beginning. From a box on the wall, a voice intones, "Everyone please stand for the Pledge of Allegiance and the National Anthem." That feat accomplished, attendance is taken and sent to the Main Office while daily announcements issue from the PA system. A bell rings, opening exercises are over and the day has begun.

With varying degrees of similarity, this scene is replayed in schools throughout our nation on a daily basis. Although they may run smoothly most of the time, there is always the possibility of students walking around during the Pledge, attendance failing to be taken or reported inaccurately or necessary information "missed," because several students were talking during the announcements. Let's look at three methods that teachers have used to work effectively with those opening exercises.

First, make certain there is enough time for students to get ready for opening exercises before they officially begin. If you announce, let us say, the Pledge and immediately begin to recite it, you will be a good deal into it before the last student is standing, with shuffling feet and scraping desks. Wait *until* everyone is standing and attentive before beginning.

Next, if you want to make certain that all procedures in those opening exercises are followed by all students, here's a simple method: Keep the class standing until everything is done. If, for example, the entire class is required to stand until the Pledge and/or National Anthem are completed, attendance is taken and recorded, all forms and/or papers are turned in or given out, and morning announcements are made, you will be *amazed* at how quickly they can get done—and how efficiently! Try this method and see how well it works.

Finally, you might want to put the routines in the hands of student committees. There might, for example, be one or two students in charge of the Pledge of Allegiance, another small committee who does nothing but take attendance, and yet a third committee whose job is to pass out and collect the materials that are always being sent home with students. The kids placed on these committees should be responsible students, and it must be apparent that you back them with your authority.

With some forethought and good organization, you can make those opening exercises run efficiently and smoothly for everyone involved.

WRITING ON THE BLACKBOARD

In our experience, we have rarely met a kid who didn't enjoy, look forward to and volunteer for writing on the black (or green or chalk) board. Indeed, on some levels the very asking for volunteers to write on the board is enough to engender a sea of hands all waving wildly.

But writing on the blackboard can produce problems as well. Who will write in what section? Where's the chalk? I can't find an eraser! Should I erase this? Harry's writing on my board! I got chalk dust on my black sweater! Surely, there must be some method of allowing your kids to write on the blackboard and keep the process smooth-running and beneficial for all those involved.

One of the most effective methods comes from a teacher who simply divided the available blackboard space among the children in her room. She then constructed the sheet in **Figure 8-1**. You will notice that it shows the section of the board and then lists the names of the students who will use that section when they are called on to write. All the teacher has to do is to make certain that not more than two from any one section are called to the board at a time. There is no more arguing about who will write where or who uses what space. Once assigned, this is their space for the school year.

Moreover, the particular section of blackboard is also their *responsibility*. That means that *they* are responsible for seeing to it that *their section* is erased properly, has sufficient chalk, erasers and any other needed materials. This could even extend to making certain that the board is washed on a regular basis.

Students still have the enjoyment and practice of writing on the blackboard, but the responsibility for all the attendant difficulties is now placed squarely in the hands of the students using it.

It saves a great deal of time and trouble.

THE HALL PASS

We doubt that anyone has ever chronicled the reasons students give for wanting to leave the classroom and venture forth into the corridors of the school, but certainly the list must run to the tens of thousands. There is not a teacher anywhere who has not been besieged with requests to go see another teacher, use the telephone to call home and various other locations, go to the office for one thing or another—all of which require the student's passage through the halls of the school.

At least some of those requests are legitimate, and if you stopped everything to write out a full-paper pass for each student, you would soon be doing little else. Let's look at something that effectively addresses this problem.

The suggestion is to have *one* hall pass. We are not indicating that this hall pass serves as a lavatory pass. Lavatory passes are a separate issue and will be addressed in "Passes to the Lavatory" (page 167). Here we are speaking of *one* pass to be used when a student must go out into the halls, such as to a locker, to the office or on an errand to another teacher.

Make the pass out of a durable material and carve, etch or write with indelible marker all the information needed, as seen on the example in **Figure 8-2**. Make this of wood or masonite, and make it large enough that any student will have to *carry* it and *cannot* put it in a pocket or purse and subsequently forget all about it. That keeps it from getting lost.

Finally, establish a policy that *no* student is *ever* in the hall without a pass and only one student may use the pass at any one time. Certainly a student may go to his locker, but if the pass isn't there, he will have to wait until it is returned before he can leave.

Under these conditions, the hall pass is quickly relegated to use by those who legitimately *need* to use it, and it saves the teacher considerable time and frustration as well.

PASSES TO THE LAVATORY

You are in the middle of a lesson that you are particularly enthusiastic about, and you call on a student whose hand is raised (possibly to have some point clarified in this wonderful learning experience). But all the student does is drone, "May I go to the lavatory?" Few things rankle teachers more. What a letdown! What an interruption both in time and in the rhythm of the lesson!

Nonetheless, most teachers we know would never deny the use of the lavatory to a student who asks. To do so might well be to invite a situation that would be totally unacceptable to everyone, and no one wants that. Surely, there must be a way to handle the lavatory situation without the undue interruption of the class.

In the last discussion, we talked about using a Hall Pass to help control students leaving the room to move in the hallways. With modification, the same technique will work for the lavatories.

Take five 3×5-inch index cards, staple them together around the edges, and with permanent marker, write the needed information on them. **Figure 8-3** shows a Girl's Lavatory Pass for our class for use during the month of November. Naturally, there is a Boy's pass as well. Use a different colored index card and/or colored ink for it, if possible. In your class, the teacher, month and room will change accordingly.

You now establish the same policy you did in the last discussion. Only one girl (or boy) on a lavatory pass at one time, and only when the pass is *in*. With this understanding, a student need *never* interrupt a lesson to ask to use the lavatory. If the pass is there, students may merely take and use it. If it is not, then they will have to wait. Naturally, should an emergency situation arise, you can suspend these rules. But most of the time, they function perfectly in saving time while effectively handling the situation.

These passes are made of index cards so that, at the end of the month, they may be cut up and thrown away and new ones made for the next month. You will understand why when you see how scrungy they become after a month's use in the school's lavatories.

THE VISITOR IN THE CLASSROOM

Teaching is *not* an endeavor in which you and your class are tossed into a classroom around September, the doors chained, and no one let in or out until late May or June of the following year. Indeed, teaching your class involves times and situations both inside and outside the classroom, with students and adults arriving and departing. Sooner or later, there will be some visitors in your classroom.

Let's face it. We all want to make a good impression on visitors and show our class in the best possible light. Let's examine two ways in which we can accomplish that goal.

First, one teacher suggests forming a Hospitality Committee. This is a group of responsible students who take over whenever there is a visitor in the classroom. The list in **Figure 8-4** details what actions members of this committee will take when a visitor comes to observe and/or be part of the class. As you can see, the actions listed are aimed at seeing to it that the visitor knows what is going on, is relatively comfortable and has everything necessary to participate in the class should that be desired.

This idea is particularly useful and time-saving if you anticipate a fair number of visitors over the course of a school year, such as parents, class mothers or volunteer grandparents visiting the class on a weekly basis. Your student Committee will soon become proficient, and each and every visitor in your classroom will be handled effectively.

If you do not anticipate visitors on that frequent a basis, you might want to appoint a single student to the task. Familiarize that student with the procedures once and then review them about once a month if there has been no opportunity to try them out. When a visitor does arrive, you might want to slip the paper in **Figure 8-4** to the student to act as a reminder.

Either way, each visitor to your classroom can have a pleasant and profitable experience in an efficient manner and without any substantial interruption of the normal classroom routine.

EMERGENCY PREPAREDNESS

The infamous Murphy's Law states that, "Anything that can go wrong, will go wrong." Unfortunately, that applies to the classroom as well as to society as a whole. The longer you teach, the closer you come to the time when that emergency situation appears at the door of your classroom demanding to be handled immediately.

There may be nothing you can do to prevent the emergency from happening, but you can do several things that can be done to prepare in advance for the happening. Let's look at some of them.

The first suggestion is to keep all emergency materials in *one place*. Perhaps it is a drawer of the file cabinet, a shelf in the closet or even a drawer of your desk, but *all* emergency materials go there and *only there*. This might include first aid materials, emergency lesson plans, special procedure lists and directions and the like. Then, tell several colleagues and at least several responsible students where that place is. In the event of an emergency situation, you have *one* place to go, and if you are not present, then someone would know where those materials were located.

Another suggestion is to *clearly post* all emergency procedures. This might include procedures for fire drills (see "The Fire Drill," page 169), any type of evacuation drill and even something like reporting to the school nurse. They might be posted permanently on a bulletin board or taped to a wall where all can see them for further reference.

Finally, in addition to all of the preceding suggestions, mark a day each month of the school year on your personal calendar. On that day, review any and all emergency procedures with your class. With the passage of time, we all tend to forget things, and our students are no exception. If we are reminded periodically, then the information or procedures will be fresh in everyone's mind and, should a situation arise, it can be handled efficiently.

Remember, you only need an emergency situation to happen *once* to be thankful for having taken the time and effort to prepare for it.

THE FIRE DRILL

We have all gone through the evacuation of the school for a fire drill. On a green afternoon in late spring, it can be a refreshing respite in the day's activities. Unfortunately, it can also be a grand headache if a class has not been properly prepared for the activity.

Schools and individual teachers have been criticized for such things as leaving lights on and windows and doors open (all of which would help an actual fire to grow), and failing to bring class records out of the building (very necessary if the fire were real). Even though a fire drill is a "right-now" situation, you can still follow certain procedures to make the fire drill much more effective.

One very effective key to that preparedness is to use the sheet in **Figure 8-5**. This is to be filled out with names of students in your class. If you have more than one class, cut off the top part (map and exit directions) and post that. Then make out a bottom part for each class, cut that out and post it around or at the bottom of the top part. Of course, the route will be specific to your classroom.

Notice that not only is the route explained in words, but it is shown in a simple and easy-to-follow map. Every chore attendant to a fire drill is listed along with the names of the students responsible for it. In short, all necessary actions by the class and individuals are covered.

The same injunctions that applied in the previous discussion on emergency preparedness apply here as well. Any procedure, even one that is prominently posted, needs to be reinforced. Until there have been several fire drills and the procedure has become all but automatic, you will need to go over them with your class.

Being prepared certainly gives us the advantage in any situation such as a fire drill.

STUDENTS WHO ARE MISSING WORKSHEETS

A child may have been absent, out of the room to the lavatory, at the Nurse's or Main Office, late to school, in Guidance, on an errand for you or not present for any one of a number of legitimate reasons when you passed out those worksheets or supplemental papers. Whatever the cause, the fact remains that one or more students are missing worksheets necessary for the unit you are currently teaching.

Supplying the "paperless" students with their worksheets can be highly time consuming. You must often search through a file cabinet or a stack of mixed papers after you have determined which ones are missing and try to find the ones required. If several students are involved, it becomes more complicated and takes longer. Let's look at a good suggestion that handles this problem.

First, make half again as many as you think you need. If you need 50, for example, run off 75. This accounts for lost sheets as well as for those who never receive them. Any that are left over may be saved for following years, so they don't go to waste. Next, never put the worksheets away until you are finished using them and they are no longer required. After worksheets have been given out to the class, place the leftovers on a table at the front of the room. If there is more than one sheet, overlap them so that the title and/or number of each will be visible. Returning students or students who may have lost certain sheets can now go directly to that table and get whatever is required without having to disturb you or the rest of the class.

Finally, you might want to establish sign-out sheets as in **Figure 8-6**. This tells you which student took what and could help you identify the "chronic" forgetter of materials. A student could be placed in charge of this sheet.

THE LEARNING MATERIALS TRUST FUND

We know a teacher who once drove all the way to school before it occurred to her that she was not wearing the eyeglasses that she had worn daily for the last 20 years. The point is that anyone can forget practically anything on occasion. If this applies to us as teachers, it applies equally well to our students who many times forget to bring certain learning materials to class.

Were it one student, once in while, it would present little or no problem at all. If, however, you have a class of kids who forget learning materials a great deal of the time or, for a variety of reasons (socioeconomic and otherwise) do not have materials to carry around, you might want to approach the problems by establishing a Learning Materials Trust Fund.

This is a classroom "bank" in which, instead of money, the commodity exchanged is a Learning Material. This Trust Fund will make "loans" to students of textbooks pencils, pens, notebooks, and the like. Records are kept of all transactions.

Figure 8-7 shows a typical "Passbook," which each student gets. Passbooks are filled out by the student borrowing from the Fund and the students who are handling the transactions of that day. As you can see, it details the who, what and when of the "loan." Lent materials are expected to be returned, and if not returned at the end of the day some penalty may be assessed by the teacher or the Fund Administrators.

Of course, teacher supervision shall always be present to make certain that no penalty is punitive and that loans are made equally to all.

While certainly not for every classroom or for every situation, this method can be particularly effective in situations where materials may not be readily available to students.

STUDENTS WITHOUT LEARNING MATERIALS

Everyone forgets something occasionally. The key word, of course, *occasionally*. Any student can "forget" to bring a text, a pen, a notebook a pencil—on occasion. That's handled quite easily, as we saw in the previous disucssion. When, however, forgetting occurs on an almost daily basis, where the student is unprepared to work virtually every day, then it may be safely assumed that a problem exists.

We are further assuming that we are dealing with children who *will not* rather than *cannot* bring such materials to class. If they will not, then perhaps a little special attention is warranted. The student's willful action may be symptomatic of other behavioral problems needing investigation.

The offending student should be isolated somewhere where there is sufficient time to carry out the activity. Give the student the sheet in **Figure 8-8** and provide the time to fill it out as completely as possible. You will notice that a response of "I don't know" is not an acceptable answer.

After the sheet has been completely filled out, you and the student go over it together. At this time, the teacher should keep stressing the reasons given by the student for the continual forgetting of materials. This entire process often makes such an impression on the chronic offender that there is an immediate improvement.

Once again, this process is for the chronic offender whose continued forgetting of learning materials is causing a distraction for you and the class. The attention given to the offender in that case will definitely go a long way toward solving the problem.

BULLETIN BOARD MANAGEMENT (I)

Bulletin boards are wonderful inventions. They display information, allow for artistic expression, provide a common ground for sharing student work or special projects and have a host of other uses too numerous to list here. Often, our question is not one of what to do with them, but how to manage them so that we use them to their maximum advantage.

Several teachers who have worked with bulletin boards for many years have some suggestions worth our consideration.

You might try dividing a bulletin board into sections as you need them. Some sections that have been used by other teachers include Personal, Messages, Me and My World, The World Of English (or Math or Science), What You Should Know, How to . . ., and so on. If you wished, these sections could be suggested by a student committee or merely allocated by you. Try for a mix of sections that would display needed school information (fire drill procedures, grading system, bus schedules), personal student work (compositions, personal coat of arms, "This Is Me"), and something to help learning (definitions of terms, posters, learning stations).

You might also like to set several students the task of developing each of these sections. These students would be responsible for researching an appropriate board for their section, preparing a sketch or plan for your approval, obtaining materials and scheduling time for putting it up, maintaining it and taking it down and storing it for future use. This task might go to the same students for the entire school year, or it could be rotated so that everyone in the class gets a chance to work on the bulletin board.

Personally, we like that last suggestion, because the more students who can work on the bulletin board, the more that bulletin board belongs to the entire class. Once it is "theirs," they will use it, care for it and see to it that it becomes a part of the classroom in which they can all take justifiable pride.

BULLETIN BOARD MANAGEMENT (II)

Bulletin boards are like textbooks in that some of them have a greater effect on our students than others. Periodically, at least in our district, the textbooks we use are evaluated for their effectiveness. Those that, in the opinion of the educators who should know, no longer perform adequately are targeted for replacement. Perhaps we would save some time and effort if we adopted the same process for our bulletin boards.

Some bulletin boards are so spectacular that you want to frame them and hang them in an art gallery. Some are even three-dimensional with stuffed birds flying out at us or hands reaching forth to invite us into the picture. While these "Wonders" are certainly indicative of a great deal of time and sometimes loving effort that have been put into them, the fact that they are elaborate does not automatically ensure that they are effective.

Figure 8-9 presents a Bulletin Board Evaluation Form. It attempts to give you some criteria for deciding whether or not you wish to use that particular bulletin board again. You critique the bulletin board while it is still on display. Then place the form in your file cabinet. In the future, you will be able to determine whether the bulletin board is worth the time and effort to recreate it.

The suggestion is that you fill in the first part, including the rough sketch, since you are in the best position to know how it was put together. Then, get a colleague to complete the remainder of the form for you. The reason for this is that you will need an *objective* opinion of its effect on students and its worth educationally. If we spend six or seven hours cutting, planning, pasting and painting, we can guarantee you that we would hardly be in a position to *objectively* assess our work. Get someone else to do it.

Months or even years from now, when you are looking for an appropriate bulletin board, this Bulletin Board Evaluation Sheet will serve you well.

KEEPING TEXTBOOKS IN REASONABLY GOOD SHAPE

In private schools, students may be required to purchase their textbooks. If a book is yours, then whatever use you choose to make of it is fine. In public education, however, where texts are literally lent to students to use for the school year, remember that another student is expected to use the same book next year. For that reason alone, the book being used must be kept in reasonably good condition.

This is often easier preached than practiced. If you have experience with kids in a school setting, then you know that textbook abuse runs rampant. Books are thrown into lockers, used as flyswatters, pounded, pummeled and persecuted. Keeping textbooks in a reasonably good condition can be a full-time chore.

A book survives better if it is covered. *You* set the example, by making certain that all your books have a cover. Set a reasonable time and then assess a penalty if student texts are not covered. Stick to it and don't take excuses. If you have set the example for yourself, then it is reasonable to expect the same thing from your students.

Next, if a textbook is "lost" by a student and you find it or it is returned to you, never merely give it back. *Always* do something to impress on the student that a text must be "cared for" and not left around carelessly to be lost. This might mean a detention, explaining in writing how and why the text was lost, a formal letter requesting its return and the like. Whatever it is, it should impress students with the necessity for keeping a tight grip on their texts.

Finally, apply the same philosophy to textbooks that you see being abused. A text that you see carelessly thrown on the floor, lying bent back in the middle or being used as third base in an impromptu ball game should not only be brought strongly to the attention of the offender, but some compensation for the abusive behavior should be forthcoming at the discretion of the teacher.

It requires perseverance, but if we keep at it, we can manage to keep those texts in reasonably good condition for the children who will use them in the future.

ASSESSING TEXTBOOK CONDITION

Eventually, the school year comes to an end, and those textbooks lent to students for a school year's use must be turned in to be distributed to a new set of students in the fall. Of course, it is to be expected that normal and reasonable use of the book will have affected the book's condition. When a book was issued new, however, and returns with its cover slashed and pages missing, that is well beyond the parameters of "normal use." In most school systems, the person who determines book condition and basically assesses whether the wear and tear has been excessive is the teacher.

Sometimes it is easy, as in the case of a new book's being returned in an unusable condition. More often, it becomes a matter of debate. Particularly if there is a fine associated with excessive wear, a student or parents may argue that the teacher's assessment was too punitive. What do you answer to that?

Your answer lies in establishing some objective criteria for your judgment. **Figure 8-10** presents a set of criteria used by one department in a particular school. Certainly, the form should be adapted to your circumstances. When judged against some established criteria, argument is kept to a minimum and a great deal of time is saved.

How do you establish this criteria? Decide on how many stages you wish. Let's say five stages (as in **Figure 8-10**) are required. Look through your textbooks and find five books that adequately reflect the stages you have in mind. Set them on a table and merely describe each one. That, or so we are advised, is how the criteria sheet in **Figure 8-10** was established. Certainly it is a quick and relatively easy way of getting objective criteria.

If this does take a little time at the outset, it will be more than compensated by the time *not* spent in arguments over subjective evaluation of textbook condition.

CHECKLIST FOR ROUTINE MANAGEMENT

A college student interested in education once visited our school for a day. At the end of that time, she was asked what impressed her the most. "It's the way you teachers handle what goes on in your classrooms," she answered. "I had no idea that you did so much in addition to teaching. How do you know what to do next?"

Certainly, that student had a good deal of perception and insight. We doubt if many teachers fully realize the extent of what we do in school each day. When we do, we often reiterate her question, "How do we know what to do next?"

Frankly, most of us have little trouble with that daily routine. We don't think about it. We just do it; it becomes a part of us. It does not follow, however, that our routine is necessarily a part of anyone else, particularly the person who may be called in to substitute for us, be it for a period or an entire school day.

That's where something like the all-purpose form in **Figure 8-11** comes in handy. If it looks simple, that's because it is. Along the left-hand side, you list your daily routine in the order in which it is handled. If you wished to elaborate on any aspect of that routine, you have space to the right to do that. You might even want to include the times for an activity such as recess or snack time.

Once filled out (and that will take very little time), it reminds you of your routine and will be a positive "road map" for anyone who has to take over your schedule, whether for a few minutes or an entire day. Should your schedule change, this all-purpose form is very easily amended.

This convenient form should be included in your emergency lesson plans to provide a good deal of comfort and guidance to your substitute.

< Window	BLACKBOARD			Door >
1.	2.	3.	4.	5.
ROW 1 (window)	ROW 2	ROW 3	ROW 4	ROW 5 (door)
Jenny	Rosa	Tai	Eric B	Jonathan
Craig	Leslie	Bill G.	Jean	Andrew
Sean	Christine	Kristy	Karen A.	John T.
Mai Li	Eric K.	Steven	Michael	Sue
Bill W.	Stephanie	John P.	Cory	Karen K.

Figure 8-1
Blackboard Assignment Plan

HALL PASS

ROOM # _____

Teacher: _____

Only ONE person may use this pass at any given time.

Figure 8-2
Hall Pass (Sample)

GIRLS Lavatory Pass

_____

(month)

Room #___ -- Periods _, _, _, _, _

_____

Teacher's Signature:

Figure 8-3
Lavatory Pass (Sample)

HOSPITALITY COMMITTEE

When a visitor enters our room during a lesson, the following people will take the action(s) described:

_____ will find a seat for our visitor and see to it that he or she is comfortable, hanging up coats and storing packages as needed.

_____ will get the visitor a copy of the textbook being used and any other worksheets or learning materials in use; supply a pencil or pen as needed.

_____ will quietly sit next to our visitor and softly explain what we are doing, the page number being used, and the requirements of the class.

_____ will, about five minutes after the visitor arrives, quietly check to see if there is anything else our visitor needs or wants and will supply it if possible.

Figure 8-4
Visitor-in-Classroom Criteria

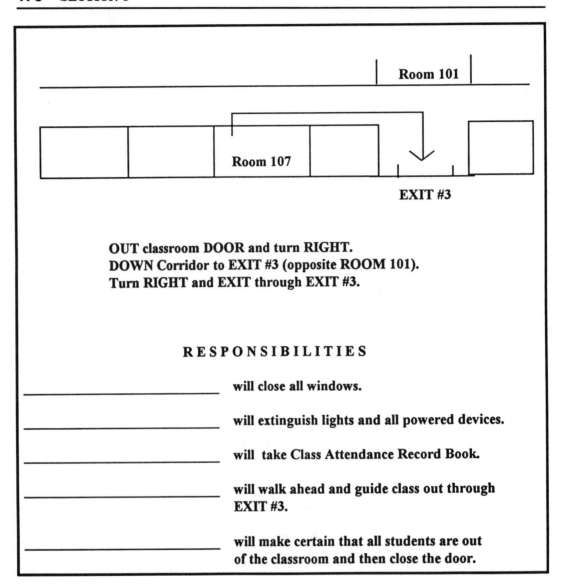

OUT classroom DOOR and turn RIGHT.
DOWN Corridor to EXIT #3 (opposite ROOM 101).
Turn RIGHT and EXIT through EXIT #3.

RESPONSIBILITIES

_____ will close all windows.

_____ will extinguish lights and all powered devices.

_____ will take Class Attendance Record Book.

_____ will walk ahead and guide class out through EXIT #3.

_____ will make certain that all students are out of the classroom and then close the door.

Figure 8-5
Fire Drill Planning Sheet

WORKSHEET SIGN-OUT		
Student	*Date*	*Worksheet(s) Needed*

Figure 8-6
Worksheet Sign-Out Form

STUDENT: _____

LEARNING MATERIALS TRUST FUND

"P A S S B O O K"

Date	Item Loaned	Returned

Figure 8-7
Learning Materials Trust Fund Passbook

NAME:_____ DATE:_____

Answer ALL of the following questions. Use additional paper if necessary. Answer each question fully. Do not write, "I don't know."

1. What does the term "LEARNING MATERIALS" mean?

2. Give at least five examples of a "LEARNING MATERIAL."

3. Why is it necessary to bring "LEARNING MATERIALS" with you to class?

4. How many times did you forget your textbook in the last month?

5. Why is it necessary for you to bring that textbook to class?

6. What are you going to do to remember to bring that textbook from now on?

7. Overall, how many times did you forget any learning material in the past month?

8. What do you intend to do about that?

9. Why do you forget to bring learning materials so often?

10. Construct a plan that will help you to bring these materials to class on a regular basis.

Figure 8-8
Chronic Offender Worksheet

BULLETIN BOARD EVALUATION FORM

TEACHER: _____

Dates Used: _____ **Room:** _____

Grade Level: _____ **Bulletin Board Title:** _____

Time Needed to Construct: _____

Materials Needed: _____
_____
_____

Special Features: _____
_____
_____

Good Points: _____
_____

Drawbacks: _____
_____

Lesson Taught by Bulletin Board: _____
_____

Students' Reaction: _____
_____

Would You Do This Bulletin Board Again? _____ **Why or Why Not?** _____
_____

Sketch of Bulletin Board:

Figure 8-9
Bulletin Board Evaluation Form

TEXTBOOK CONDITION CRITERIA

NEW --   As it came from the publisher; pristine; no previous use.

EXCELLENT --   Slight signs of wear, but cover unmarked and pages "crisp"; unmarked in any way, but some signs of use around edges of cover; used once or twice previously.

GOOD --   Deeper signs of wear; some marks on cover and some pages crimped or slightly dirty; color somewhat faded with dust and time; possibly some marks on pages; used three or four times previously.

FAIR --   Deep signs of wear; corners bent and pages frayed around corners and edges; book has "unclean" appearance; marks on pages and cover; used five times previously.

POOR --   Just barely usable; loose pages and cover; pages and cover marked and scarred; book appears "dirty"; possibly missing or ripped pages; used six or more times previously.

Figure 8-10
Textbook Condition Criteria

Teacher: _____

For the school year _____ to _____

SCHEDULE	TIME FRAME	COMMENT

Figure 8-11
Routine Management Checklist

TIME-SAVING STEPS IN HOME-SCHOOL COOPERATION

On an illuminated sign outside a middle school in our area is the legend, "Dedicated Teachers + Motivated Students + Supportive Parents = SUCCESS." Ask teachers, and they will tell you there is nothing to argue about in that statement. When teachers, students and the home cooperate, even the hardest problems stand an excellent chance of being solved and solved quickly.

This section will explore the home-school cooperation that is such a necessary component of student success. Let's look at some practical ways of utilizing the formula that works so well—positive contact with the home and managing parental conferences to make certain the home is informed and involved.

POSITIVE PARENTAL CONTACT (I)

In previous sections, we have stressed the importance of establishing a positive parental contact as quickly as possible in the school year. We even suggested some positive ways in which that contact can be established. A parent who has been approached in a positive manner is a parent who is on your side, and that can only be to your advantage throughout the year.

We hope this doesn't sound simplistic, but one of the surest ways to get parents on your side and assure positive parental contact is simply to make friends with them. Let us share with you several suggestions from fellow educators on how to achieve that goal.

You could start by inviting parents to be chaperones on class trips. It has been our experience that many are anxious to go, and many are willing to pay their own way if expense is involved. The class trip provides a good chance to get to know parents on a personal basis and establish a mutually beneficial rapport.

Next, you could use special occasions in the classroom or school to confide in parents and get them on your side. If you have a class play, presentation or party, you might want to telephone several parents and share your concerns that everything runs smoothly and according to schedule, thereby enlisting their cooperation and aid and establishing a positive working relationship with them. Certainly, you will get all the help you need to supervise or simply to help where needed in these situations.

Finally, don't forget the simple amenities. A "thank you" note or a follow-up phone call expressing your gratitude for the parent's cooperation and help can work wonders in establishing that positive relationship. Everyone likes to be acknowledged when they have done something helpful, and parents are no exception. The note need not be effusive, just genuine.

Making a friend out of a parent is certainly one of the finest methods of ensuring positive parental contact.

POSITIVE PARENTAL CONTACT (II)

Certainly, many teachers have excellent ideas for establishing positive parental contact with the home, but contact need not be on a one-time basis. Indeed, once positive contact has been made, try to maintain that relationship over the remaining school year.

Figure 9-1 is an example of just such a positive rapport builder. You might consider establishing a class newsletter that goes to the parents of every student in the class. This "newsletter" (you can call it whatever you wish) would go to the home on a regular basis—once a month, once a marking period or at whatever intervals you feel you can handle.

It need not be a long and involved endeavor, either. A single page of standard 8.5×11-inch paper, printed on one side, can be just as effective as a four-page tabloid. What it contains is more important than its size.

This newsletter should reflect your class and your students and, to really build positive parental contact, the child who will take this paper home. If you look at **Figure 9-1**, you will see a very short paragraph about a student, Eric Folesome (purely fictional), and what he has accomplished in class. What if that one paragraph were different on each newsletter that went home? What if each newsletter contained a paragraph about a different child until every child had his or her paragraph of recognition?

This can be accomplished by using a computer with word processing capabilities. If the basic newsletter is entered into a file, then it is a relatively easy matter to delete or amend one paragraph and replace it with another. This is particularly true if all that needs to be changed is a name and a grade or project title.

This will take some effort, but the positive parental rapport established could save you a great deal of effort later on.

POSITIVE PARENTAL CONTACT (III)

Education should never be a 12-year war between the school and the home fought over the battleground of the child. When the home and school fight, the child loses. When the home and school cooperate, the child comes out the winner. Often, gaining that cooperation can be a time-consuming and frustrating task that tests the patience of the teacher involved.

Several teachers have suggested one way that rarely fails to gain support and establish rapport: Ask the parent for advice.

Figure 9-2 represents a letter to a parent asking for advice on establishing a plan to help a student. Note that the letter does not beg or sound dictatorial, mandating the parent's actions. Rather, it takes the tack that the parent is the person who knows the child best. There is a problem and both of you are certainly concerned about it. Perhaps the parent might offer some advice that could be helpful.

You will notice that it does not say you will use the advice given; you are merely asking for input. Consequently, unusable or possibly detrimental advice need not be implemented.

On rare occasion you may receive an answer along the lines of, "You're the teacher; don't ask me to do your job!" While this is rare, it does happen.

Most of the time, however, you'll receive a positive response or a parental suggestion that works toward solving the child's problem.

If nothing else, your asking for advice will go a long way toward building positive parental rapport, and you may be pleasantly surprised at the results as well.

PARENTAL CONTACT RECORDKEEPING

How many times throughout this book have we suggested keeping some sort of record of what you do? We have made the suggestion often because it is so important. When controversy arises, as it inevitably will, a written record of who did what and when it was done, can be a bright torch in a dark night. That same philosophy applies to *all* contact between the teacher and the parents.

One teacher uses a "Parental Contact Record Sheet," as in **Figure 9-3**. While this form is extremely simple, it can be of tremendous value when used properly.

Run off a number of these sheets and keep them handy. The first time you contact the home, take one of them and fill in the student information at the top. Then fill in the date, the reason for contact and the outcome of the contact in the proper spaces after meeting, calling or writing the parent. File it, and keep it until the next time you must contact the home. Take it out then and make your next entry. Make a new entry on the sheet each time you contact the student's home.

Each time you initiate a home contact for a new student, begin a new sheet. Soon you will have a complete, yet separate, record of every parental contact for each student with whom you have dealt.

How necessary is this parental contact recordkeeping? Let's hope you never need to document actions relative to a student. However, you need be required to do so only once, to see the benefits of good recordkeeping.

INVOLVING GUIDANCE IN PARENTAL CONTACT

Sometimes we cannot handle the situation alone. Perhaps we have tried positive parental contact and made "all the right moves," only to find our efforts thwarted at every turn. If this is the case, seek help. Often a source of help comes from the Guidance setup in your school.

The home may be more disposed to listen to the Guidance Counselor than to the classroom teacher. Parents may know the counselor from contacts with siblings in the school or perceive a call from Guidance as having greater authority than a phone call from a teacher.

If our ultimate goal is to help our students, then use whatever works.

Toward that end, you might try using the form in **Figure 9-4**. If you are going to involve Guidance, then it stands to reason that Guidance must be well-informed to perform properly. A thoroughly filled-out form such as **Figure 9-4** can document the problem and what you have done, serve as a permanent record of your actions if they are questioned later and function as a hard fact reminder to Guidance to use in any subsequent meetings or phone conversations.

Of course, you could adapt that form to include or exclude any appropriate information, but with this printed copy, Guidance will be better prepared to act in your behalf for the positive welfare of your student.

THE NOTE OR ITEM SENT HOME

Here's an experience we have all shared: Something happens in class, and you hastily jot a note to the student's parent. You give it to the student with the injunction to have it signed and returned the next day. The item may be a note from you, a test, a composition or a confiscated note, but it is important that the parent see the item and that you have verification that it was seen.

What happens the next day if the item is *not* returned? The child may tell you that he forgot it, lost it on the way home or that it was eaten by the family dog. You may be informed that one or both parents are on extended vacation in Zanzibar. Or you may receive the note signed with a highly questionable signature. When any of those things happens, you are going to follow up, and if the student becomes a chronic offender in this area, then you can try some techniques.

Let's assume that the item meant to reach home is a note.

You can give the note to the child to take home, and then call the student's home without the student's knowledge and tell the home that the note *should be* forthcoming. This is *extremely effective* provided you have built a positive rapport with the home and you are working *with* the parent for the good of the child.

Another suggestion: Send mail to the home in a *nonschool* envelope, particularly if it is to be mailed to a student you know might intercept your communication. Also, require some sort of return verification on all materials sent home through the mail.

Finally, and only where applicable and feasible, you might try giving the note to someone else in the school who has contact with the offender's home, keeping that fact secret from the offending student. Quite often, this has assured that the item went to the parents. Of course, you must use your judgment and personal knowledge of the people involved in determining if this would work in your case.

THE NOTE OR ITEM UNRETURNED

What happens if all the techniques mentioned in the previous discussion simply do not work? What happens if the child simply refuses to hand it back or keeps coming up with excuses? He protests that it *was* seen, and it *was* signed—he just keeps forgetting to bring it. What if this scenario has played for several days?

One teacher employs a unique approach that seems to work well for him: First, set a reasonable time limit for the return of the item or note. When that time has expired and the note is still unreturned, arrange for the student to report to you in the Main Office or Guidance Office during your preparation time or professional period. You may personally inform other teachers about what you are doing, but often a simple note will suffice.

When the student arrives, give him or her the script in **Figure 9-5**. Have the student read it several times to make certain he or she is reading it correctly, and then dial the student's home and have the child read the script to his mother, father or guardian. When he or she has come to the part about putting you on the line, you must be ready to take over, but by then both the student and the home should understand the point.

As you read the script in **Figure 9-5,** you should feel free to amend it in whatever way best suits your class and the limits you set for the return of the note or item. The script places the responsibility squarely on the student and the home, and the child must face up to his or her lack of care or concern.

This tactic not only brings in the missing item or note, but acts as a deterrent to the student repeating this behavior in the future.

GETTING A HANDLE ON PARENTAL PHONE CALLS

The advent of the telephone has changed the face of education. Now, there is instant communication available between the home and the school. If parent and teacher cannot meet face to face, they can certainly meet ear to ear. In most cases, the telephone is a quick and efficient method of handling those problems that pop up on a day-to-day basis.

What if you want to call a parent who isn't in during the day? One teacher suggests calling between six and seven in the evening. You will most likely interrupt their dinner, but the chances are good that you will reach the parent. The same is true of calling around seven in the morning, before the family has started its day. If all else has failed to get results, these tactics may succeed.

If, on the other hand, you, as a teacher, are deluged by parental calls to the school each demanding that you return the call immediately, then you can do something to handle this situation as well. If this is the case with you, try selecting one time during the school day when you do not have a class or a duty. *That time and only that time* will you be available to return phone calls. Most parents will honor that, especially if you publish that information in a note to each home.

Thereafter, make certain that you adhere to it. If you have too many calls to handle during one such period, then those that remain will have to wait until the next day. Soon, the information about the time that you are available will begin to spread and the number of calls that may be effectively handled should fall to a reasonable level.

MANAGEMENT OF PARENTAL CONFERENCES (I)

Certainly, little problems, as well as some of larger proportions, may be handled through the note sent home or the telephone call to the parent. Sometimes, however, this is simply not enough, with the notes and phone calls accomplishing little or nothing, when nothing else will do but a face-to-face meeting between the teacher or teachers and the parents.

When that happens, here is an excellent method of saving a great deal of time while ensuring that everyone understands exactly what has taken place.

First, give every person involved in the conference a copy of the sheet in **Figure 9-6**. The sheet is fairly self-explanatory, but the person in charge of the conference may wish to take a moment or two to explain it. Stress that *every person at the conference*, including the student in question, if present, must fill out a sheet.

You may allow time to fill out the sheet during the meeting or at the end. Completed sheets are handed to the person in charge of the conference or a person on whom both teacher and parent agree. A guidance counselor or a neutral third party might serve that purpose.

This third party takes the sheets and, using a fresh sheet, writes down the consensus of what has been said, stressing particularly any plans for future action that may have been agreed on during the conference. Any major disagreements should be noted as well. When that sheet is finished, it is reproduced and a copy given to everyone who attended the conference, including one or two copies for the file. Now, there is no question of misunderstanding since everyone has in writing exactly what is expected.

MANAGEMENT OF PARENTAL CONFERENCES (II)

No matter how well the parental conference went or how insightful and education-ally sound the solutions offered might have been, the entire thing will count for nothing if the suggestions are not implemented or if the cooperation talked about at the meeting remains nothing but talk. The suggestions made at the parental conference must be incorporated into the student's daily school life if the conference is to have value. Once the conference is over, the parent has gone home, and a few hours or even days have passed, the situation often looks different, and the plans made at the conference may not seem as necessary to implement.

That is why it is a very good tactic for the teacher to send a follow-up note to the parent shortly after the conference. An example of an effective postconference note may be seen in **Figure 9-7**. The blanks in this note should be filled in with the pertinent information and with the topics and/or plans of action that were decided on and agreed to at the conference. Filling this out and sending it home one or two days later reminds parents in a very friendly way of what they promised to do and the cooperation you expect.

Here's a time-saving suggestion: Enter **Figure 9-7** into a word processing program on your computer or the school's. Once that has been done, it becomes an easy task to change the date to have it relate to the conference at hand and print out a letter ready to be mailed. You don't have to write a new letter each time, just revise the pertinent information.

Don't sell this short. A follow-up note can go a long way toward ensuring the cooperation of the home. It brings results.

PARENT-TEACHER-STUDENT COOPERATION (I)

We all know it to be true: When teacher, parents and student are working together, few problems cannot be solved. Problems come in, however, when one or more parts of the threesome cease to work properly. When that happens, the entire effectiveness of the parent-teacher-student partnership is threatened.

Let's share a method that one teacher uses to ensure that the three-way cooperation is maintained in the days following the conference.

Figure 9-8 is a type of progress report. While virtually every school has its own version, this one is different from those normally used. First of all, this is for one subject only—your subject. Next, notice that there is nothing to "check off;" each person using the sheet is expected to make a comment before "signing off."

When the sheet is returned from the last person to fill it out, copies of it are made and one copy goes to each of the participants as well as to the Guidance Counselor or whoever was involved from the school's administration.

This document shows with 100-percent accuracy exactly what each person involved has done. Also, it serves as a clear picture of how each views the progress so far, and it can instantly tell you what real adjustments, if any, need to be made and when.

Moreover, these weekly or monthly sheets serve as a record of all the efforts you have made on the student's behalf should that verification ever be required.

This type of form may not be needed for every problem, but for those to which it does apply, it's an excellent way of keeping teacher, parent and student on track.

PARENT-TEACHER-STUDENT COOPERATION (II)

In any endeavor, someone must be in charge. Without someone in authority, any activity quickly degenerates into disorder. This applies to life in general, and it also applies to that Parent-Teacher-Student cooperative effort we detailed in the previous discussion. If it's going to work, somebody has to take control.

In most cases, that "someone" will be you, the classroom teacher. If you do all the work, however, then the student has not really benefitted from the process.

Here, then, are some suggestions for getting the student and the parent to effectively handle their share of the responsibility.

Consider a once-a-week telephone conference, perhaps in the Guidance Office, where you and the parent and child can all talk, preferably with you sitting directly across from the student. You would be amazed what a degree of honesty in the student that physical setup engenders.

Or have the student write his or her own progress report. This might be one or two paragraphs done once a week or every two weeks or monthly, as you direct. In it the student is to tell what he or she did this time period to accomplish the goals that you and the parent have set. You need not correct this; just read it. If the student's version diverges a good deal from the truth, then you can write a comment yourself or follow up this self-written progress report with a telephone call to the parent.

Finally, in truly serious cases, consider calling the parent to come in on a once-a-week basis for a month or so. Caution them that the student should not be told when this will happen, and you should vary the day of the week so that no preset schedule can be determined. All the parent does is observe. We have found that this is often enough. When the situation improves, those parental visits can become less frequent or stop entirely.

PARENTS AS CLASSROOM VOLUNTEERS

Not to belabor the point, but your class is *your* class. This means that how you decide to teach that class, within reasonable boundaries, is largely up to you. The same thing applies to the use of parents as classroom volunteers. Frankly, some teachers have complained that parents were great distractions, hindering the learning process, while others have lauded the participation of parents and count on them as we might count upon a textbook or chalkboard.

That decision will always be up to you, of course; but if you decide to try using parents as classroom volunteers, a few hints will save time and make the process easier.

First, determine what you can live with. You might want to jot down a few things you would expect of parental volunteers and some things you would not accept. Formulate these ideas into a set of criteria for parental volunteers. **Figure 9-9** is representative of one teacher and one class only, just as yours should reflect you and your class.

When asking for parental volunteers, publish this criteria list and make it very clear that if a parent cannot agree to those standards, then he or she should not volunteer. This could, of course, be phrased as diplomatically as possible, but stick to it. Possibly, you might want to include a sign-off, which states that the potential volunteer has read and agrees with the criteria.

The point is that if you are going to have parental volunteers, you should make certain that they will observe your established rules and will help you implement your plans for the education of their children. When everyone understands this and agrees to it up front, a good deal of time and trouble can be saved.

When that happens, it is your students who will benefit.

KEEPING PARENTS INFORMED

If you have ever sat in a conference and heard parents protest that something would surely have been done about their failing or disruptive child if only they had known, then you will understand the absolute necessity of keeping parents informed. For most parents, the midmarking period progress report and/or the standard report card are sufficient. In some cases, however, that is simply not enough.

Some children require closer supervision than most and a great deal more attention if they are to get value from their school experience.

For this special situation, you might want to try the form in **Figure 9-10**. You will notice that this reports to the parent from the child's point of view, and you should have the student fill it out in your presence. In the Student section, let the student write whatever he or she pleases. You will have the opportunity to add a statement of your own afterward.

What do you do with this once it has been filled out? You may make several copies of it, including one for your files and one for the Guidance Office or other agency that may be involved. Get these copies to the proper places, and send the original to the child's home.

Here, you might want to try one of the techniques we mentioned earlier to ensure that the note gets home, such as calling first or mailing it in a plain envelope.

However you do it, you now have documented evidence that the situation exists, that you are working to solve it, and that the home has been notified.

If this seems a bit "much," remember that this technique is for that "special" case where the progress report or report card just doesn't work.

CHECKLIST FOR HOME INVOLVEMENT

Teachers do their best to work with and for every student under their care. The cliche of "bending over backwards" certainly applies to the efforts of a teacher with the child who refuses to work, refuses to learn, refuses to cooperate, or refuses to allow others to learn.

In any of those cases, one of the first avenues of approach is to contact the home. Certainly, this simple expedient quickly and efficiently handles many a minor problem. Sometimes that home contact is not a one-time matter; it may be ongoing throughout the entire year.

When that happens, document all your attempts to involve the home in the situation. So much can happen and so much can go wrong, that it is not impossible to have the home accuse you of not having informed or notified them or not having followed up on a plan or course of action. Much, if not all, of this may be avoided by the use of the simple form in **Figure 9-11**.

Let's call this a checklist for home involvement. At the time of each contact, fill out the date, check off the appropriate box, and at an appropriate later time, make a short comment if you want. Those comments need not be chapters in a book; a couple of well-chosen words can be a reminder of the incident.

What you have is an ongoing record of all your attempts to involve the home in helping their child and the reaction of the home in each case. This can serve as proof of your commitment and might also trace patterns of behavior.

This differs from **Figure 9-3** by recording not only what you have done, but the outcome as well. In this case a mere check would suffice most of the time. This is geared toward the long haul.

When you need to fall back on something like this, it is well worth your effort.

The "710" EXPRESS

Mrs. Rivera's Class, Section 7-10, November Issue

"7-10ers" TO VISIT TURKEY FARM
Getting Ready for Thanksgiving

Mrs. Rivera's 7-10 class will be bundling up and going on a visit to Zigmeyer's Turkey Farm on Thursday, November 16. They will go on a tour of the place, seeing where and how turkeys are raised.

STUDENT SUCCESS FILE

Eric Folesome of section 7-10 is being given special mention in this issue. This is due to the fact that during the last month of school, Eric scored an "A" on Unit Tests in Science, Social Studies, and Language Arts. Section 7-10 congratulates Eric on this fine achievement.

Students will also get to see some fields where pumpkins are grown. Since pumpkins are also traditional for the Thanksgiving holiday, each student will be allowed to pick his or her own pumpkin to take home.

Students are advised to dress warmly for the trip.

Figure 9-1
Positive Parental Rapport Builder

Dear Mrs. Barker,

As you are aware by my recent note, Mindy is not doing all of her classwork. While we both know she has the ability to do the work, it is often only partially done or not done at all, even though sufficient time has been given.

We both understand that Mindy can do a great deal better than that, and we are, certainly, both anxious that she improve.

Frankly, I have known Mindy for a few months, while you have known her all of her life. That's why I was wondering if you had any suggestions for dealing with this problem or insights that would help us better understand the situation.

Since you know your child best, I would be most anxious and most appreciative to hear from you about this.

Working together, I know we can really help Mindy work up to her full potential.

Yours sincerely,

Donna Kincaid

Figure 9-2
Parental Advice Letter

Student: _____ Grade: _____

Homeroom: _____ Home telephone: _____

Teacher: _____ Subject/Period: _____

PARENTAL CONTACT RECORD SHEET

Date	How Contacted	Reason for Contact	Outcome of Contact

Figure 9-3
Parental Contact Record Sheet

TO: _____, Guidance
FROM: _____, Teacher
RE: _____, Student

Student Home Room _____ Home Telephone _____

Description of Problem:

How Guidance Might Become Involved:

Record of Previous Teacher Action:

Date	Action Taken	Result

Figure 9-4
Guidance Information Form

(when connection has been made)

Hello, _____,

    This is _____ and I'm calling from school. I'm all right, and everything is OK, but I'm calling from the office, and my teacher, _____, is standing here beside me.

    My teacher wants me to read something to you. Here it is:

_____ days ago, I was given _____ to take home to you. It was to be signed and returned by the next day. That was _____ days ago. As yet, I have not returned it. I have been asked _____ times by my teacher, _____, to bring it back, and as yet I have not.

    My teacher wishes to speak to you now.

(hand phone to the teacher)

Figure 9-5
Student Telephone Script

Parental conference held on (Date):_____

Subject of conference (Student):_____

Present at conference (Circle Your Name):

What is the problem:

Possible causes:

Possible solutions:

Recommended course(s) of action at present time:

Comment(s):

Figure 9-6
Parental Conference Consensus Sheet

_____ , 19 _____

Dear _____ ,

   Thank you so much for attending the conference concerning your _____ ,
_____ , *that was held on* _____ , 19 _____ .

   Not only was it good to meet and speak to you, but I am certain that _____
will really benefit from the cooperation between us.

   *As a positive reminder to us both, I have taken the liberty of outlining the suggestions
made at the conference. Here they are:*

   _____

   _____

   _____

   _____

   _____

   *Again, thank you for your cooperation and understanding. I am very hopeful of every
future success.*

                    Yours sincerely,

                    _____

Figure 9-7
Parental Conference Follow-up Note

STUDENT:_____ SUBJECT:_____
COVERING THE PERIOD FROM _____ TO _____

Please make a written comment concerning the student and subject during the time period listed above. Please sign in the space provided after the full comment has been written.

STUDENT (Please Print Name):_____

Date:_____   Student's Signature:_____

TEACHER (Please Print Name):_____

Date:_____   Teacher's Signature:_____

PARENT/GUARDIAN (Please Print Name):_____

Date:_____   Par./Guard. Signature:_____

Figure 9-8
Three-Party Progress Report

CRITERIA FOR PARENTAL VOLUNTEERS

Thank you for offering to volunteer. Below are some of the criteria for parents who volunteer to help out:

1. A schedule will be established, and it is expected that we will adhere to it. Please give notice if you cannot be here at your appointed time.
2. Check in with me when you arrive and before you leave.
3. Leave your work area clean; supervise student clean-up.
4. If there is any accident or if a child is hurt (even a very minor scratch), report it to me at once.
5. Avoid working with YOUR child ALL THE TIME. Spread yourself around; get to as many children as possible.
6. If there are ANY problems (anything at all), see me immediately; please check with me before taking any action that would take children outside the classroom or outside of the approved curriculum or textbook.
7. Please understand that ALWAYS, at ALL times, and IN EVERY WAY, YOU are deeply appreciated.

Thanks for your help.

_____, Teacher

Figure 9-9
Parental Volunteers Criteria

Student's Name:_____ Date:_____

WHAT HAPPENED IN SCHOOL TODAY?

STUDENT: Please state exactly what happened and what you did.	TEACHER: Please comment as necessary

STUDENT:_____   TEACHER:_____

Figure 9-10
Report of Incident to Parent Form

STUDENT:_____ GRADE:_____

H.R. _____ Class/Section:_____ Home Telephone:_____

Teacher:_____ Subject:_____

Date:	Incident:		Home Contact:			Home:		Comment:
	Behavioral	**Academic**	**Note**	**Phone**	**Personal**	**Response**	**None**	
	( )	( )	( )	( )	( )	( )	( )	
	( )	( )	( )	( )	( )	( )	( )	
	( )	( )	( )	( )	( )	( )	( )	
	( )	( )	( )	( )	( )	( )	( )	
	( )	( )	( )	( )	( )	( )	( )	
	( )	( )	( )	( )	( )	( )	( )	
	( )	( )	( )	( )	( )	( )	( )	

Figure 9-11
Home Involvement Checklist

SAVING TIME IN SPECIAL SCHOOL SITUATIONS

Virtually all schools run on routine, with bells and electronic tones periodically informing us that it is time to move on to the next phase of the school day. While this system works well most of the time, circumstances arise that chip away at the well-established structure. Indeed, it is in handling these special school situations that we often meet our greatest challenges.

From class parties to teacher evaluations, let's look at how educators are managing these incidents efficiently and effectively.

THE CLASS PARTY (I)

Frankly, some teachers love class parties while others view them with all the enthusiasm reserved for an afternoon of root canal work. Certainly, we have all heard about or witnessed the class party that has gotten out of hand, where students have become so keyed up that they were virtually uncontrollable. Cake and soda fly through the air. The harried teacher is left, at the end of it all, with a room that looks like the starting place for World War III. What a great deal of wasted time and trouble, especially since it doesn't have to be that way.

If you are going to have parties at all, then you would do well to set up some restrictions. If your school has an overriding set of rules concerning parties, review it with your class. If it is up to you to set the standard, a simple statement such as, "There will be no parties for individual birthdays," immediately cuts down on the number of parties and requests for parties. You might also consider publishing a calendar with a number of preset party dates (fall, winter, spring, June; all birthdays from July 1 to December 31 and then all birthdays from January 1 through June 30). You can then add the adisory that there will be no other parties—for *any reason, ever*—than those listed. Finally, all these parties should have limits attached to them for time (8th period *only*; 2:30-3:30 *only*, etc.) and place (*our classroom*; the *all-purpose room*; North end of the *cafeteria*).

Most importantly, don't handle the party by yourself. This is an excellent time to involve the parents of your students. **Figure 10-1** is an example of a note that might be sent to parents soliciting aid with an upcoming class party. Notice that it is friendly, but details exactly what is needed in terms of help from parents and suggests that, if this aid is not forthcoming, the party may be cancelled, which is not a bad principle to follow.

Finally, the day *before* the party, insist on meeting with all the parent helpers/chaperones. At this meeting, give them a "battle plan" detailing what each parent will do *before, during,* and *after* the party. If party is well planned and all parties understand what they are to do, then everyone—even you and the parents—should have a good time.

THE CLASS PARTY (II)

The class party, particularly at the elementary school level, can be a joyous occasion if it is well planned. In the previous discussion, we gave several suggestions for seeing to it that there are no deviations from the "battle plan." Now, let's look at some suggestions for dealing with the end of the party and its aftermath in a efficient and time-saving manner.

It is strongly suggested that all parties be held at the *end* of the school day. When the bell rings ending school, all the students leave the building, allowing you and your parent volunteers the time, space and freedom to clean up. That same party given, let us say, at the beginning of the school day would leave you with a dirty room to clean, as students and teachers moved into and out of the scene, and one class of sugar-filled, highly energized kids for you to *try* to control. Make the party the *last* thing in the day.

Even though they go from the party to the buses to home, and even though there may have been marvelous supervision during the affair, once the last child has consumed the last slice of cake and left the party room, you are still faced with the task of cleaning up.

Figure 10-2 is a clean-up list for a party held in school by one teacher with parental volunteers. Naturally, you would amend the list to reflect your needs. Notice, however, that every aspect of the clean-up is detailed and assigned to an adult, with you taking an active part but not the *only* part in the process. Notice also the suggestion that everyone should remain until the room is returned to proper condition for normal class activities.

If this is properly organized, and everyone does the assigned job the clean-up should take only between five and ten minutes, with the work shared equally among the people present.

THE CLASS PLAY

In many schools, the producing and/or directing of the school play is a matter of contract. This is especially true in middle and secondary schools where the play may be a full, two-act musical comedy, with a large student cast, to be presented on several evenings. In many schools, however, particularly in elementary school, the dramatic effort for the year may consist of an evening for each class in the school to produce a theatrical gem. And, of course, the director and producer of the class play is? *You!*

As director/producer, the secret of saving time and frustration is basically the same as for the class party (See the previous discussions in this section)—planning and outside help.

As teachers who have gone through this will verify, any class usually has enough parents with special skills to get the play into production. Is there a parent dance enthusiast/instructor who could volunteer for choreography? A musical parent who will be a rehearsal pianist? A director-parent who will take over one rehearsal per week? A sewing parent who will take charge of costumes? A cosmetologist parent for make-up? If you ask, you are going to find all these and more who love to see their children on stage and who are more than willing to help out if you let them know they are needed.

The notice in **Figure 10-3** does just that. Of course, you will adapt the notice to your needs, your class, and your play, but this should give you a basic starting point. Remember that *everyone* can help, and even parents who claim to have no skills can still help direct traffic backstage, keep children quiet or just provide their presence for supervision and support.

Everyone comes out a winner, you have saved yourself a good deal of time and trouble, and the play will probably be outstanding as well.

THE ART PROJECT IN THE CLASSROOM

Are you the teacher who volunteered to do the showcase across from the main office? Your class was going to do a presentation on immigration into the United States, complete with a three-foot-high model of the Statue of Liberty. That model is to be built and stored, prior to its move to the showcase, in your classroom. Now, all you need do is make certain that the art project in your classroom does not get stepped on, mutilated or destroyed, and the building of the thing does not result in paint and glue all over the walls or the loss of several class periods of instruction as the project literally "takes over."

Let's look at some suggestions for handling the art project in the classroom so that it does not get out of hand.

First, make certain you have enough supplies to complete the project once it is started. The more you run out of paint or construction paper or glue and have to send out for these items, the more behind you become, the more frustrated the builders become, and the more turmoil encompasses the classroom. Make sure, before you begin, you can finish the project.

Next, if the project is large, such as a three-foot model of the Statue of Liberty, a giant time-waster is the taking out of the materials and their storing away afterwards. An innovative solution to this comes from an art teacher who suggests getting a very large cardboard box, cutting off the top and, on a diagonal, two adjacent sides of the box. Now, in that box you place the project on which the class is working. In it you also place all the materials that are need to work on that project—glue, markers, paper, rulers, scissors and the like.

Think of the advantages: Only *one item* (the box) needs to be taken out and later put away. When it comes time to clean up (and this can be lessened by making certain that the project remains *in* the box while it is worked on if possible), all materials are put back into the box and the box is placed in a corner of the room, possibly with a sheet over it.

Try it. It really saves a great deal of trouble.

ANIMAL IN THE CLASSROOM

When it come to "war stories" among teachers, many of them revolve around the misadventures of having animals in the classroom. We are not referring to the use of animals for scientific purposes (that is a topic in and of itself). Rather, we are talking about students bringing in their pets and/or various wildlife to show the class. It may sound like a great idea, but should that animal decide to urinate on your desk, bite a child or get loose and career about a classroom of screaming children, the whole concept will seem rather less attractive. And you might possibly be facing some upset parents with legal action on their minds.

Therefore, every teacher should consider very carefully before allowing any animal into the classroom. If, however, this is not in violation of your school's policy and you should desire to allow a child to bring in an animal, there is a guideline that you should follow to avoid potential trouble in the situation.

Long before any child or parent brings an animal into your classroom, make sure they have read and signed some sort of release form such as in **Figure 10-4**. They must *clearly* understand that *they* are responsible for that animal and all that the animal does while in the school. This includes all cleaning up that may be required as well as taking responsibility for any actions (biting, scratching etc.) that the animal may take.

If the parent will not sign a release, do not allow the animal to come in. The benefits of showing the animal to the class simply do not outweigh the potential hazards.

Finally, if the animal is coming to the classroom, you would do well to invite (in fact, we would insist on the presence of) a Guidance Counselor or Administrator to witness how the situation is handled and all else that transpires.

Make certain you have covered all angles, and you will make things easier for yourself.

USING MOVIES/VIDEOS IN CLASS

At one time in our classrooms, movies were printed on 16-mm film and shown via projector on a screen or a bare wall. Times have certainly changed, and virtually all schools now have a VCR and TV monitor, some schools acquiring two or three for each grade level or department. This device has made the showing of movies on videocassette an easy and painless operation. However, the same problems we faced with movies several decades ago still apply to video today.

In regard to all movies, let us share the greatest trouble-saver we know: *Preview the movie!* Sure, it is going to take time to look at the movie beforehand. But that is nothing compared to the time you will spend explaining to angry parents or your principal or the Board of Education why you allowed your class to view something that is reserved strictly for adults and is questionable at best.

After you have previewed the video and know it is appropriate for viewing by your class, you have another problem. How do you assure that the class, in the semidarkness of the room, is actually watching the movie rather then doing homework or daydreaming about the upcoming football game with the cross-town rival?

You do this by making your audience *active* viewers. Before the movie begins, give the class a sheet such as that in **Figure 10-5**. Each viewer will answer this list of questions *during* the video and hand it in *after* the video. Now the attention of the class *has* to be focused on the presentation if they wish to get the work done. Of course, this won't guarantee that all your student will have their eyes riveted to the screen, but it does help to focus their attention.

Who knows, they just might enjoy themselves while learning, and that's education at its best!

USING THE SCHOOL LIBRARY

True education, it has been said, consists not in looking in a book to find the answer, but in knowing which book to look into. If that is true, the place we will most likely find that book is in the library. Getting students to understand how the school library functions and then to use that library is a gift that teacher can give to their students that will serve them throughout their lives.

Toward that end, we have found that most school librarians are extremely anxious that the library be *used*, and they can be a great help in introducing the library to your class. One of your first time-savers would be to meet with this person to arrange a time. An initial assignment of a sheet of simple questions (varied, of course, by the level of your class), whose answers can be found in encyclopedias and other library resources, can help familiarize students with the many benefits of the library.

Another effective tool is the use of a "Library Map." **Figure 10-6** gives a sample. Naturally, your map must reflect the floor plan of your library and its book placement. Reproduce these maps and give a copy to each student in class well *before* their trip to the actual library. The students take the map with them when they go as a group to the library and, if they have been prepared, are spared a great deal of floundering about. It saves lots of time and trouble.

Of course, you can pass out the maps with all or some of the sections unlabeled and have the students fill in that information as they "discover" it, but that is up to you and the needs of your class.

A working knowledge of libraries will benefit your students all their lives. We owe it to them to make sure they are properly introduced to this outstanding learning tool.

AWARDS TO STUDENTS

We all like to be recognized for our efforts. This applies to teachers, and it applies to our students and their parents as well. The student who has received an award literally beams with joy, and so does the proud parent. Indeed, your own experience will surely acknowledge that awards won in school are often kept, tended and cherished far beyond the school years, and they provide great pleasure for those who have received them.

Here are some suggestions from your fellow educators concerning *awards* that will help you save some time while making the most of this tool.

First of all, **Figure 10-7** may be looked upon as a sort of "All-Purpose" award form. It can be copied as is if desired and run off in quantity. You may want to print or letter in the name of your school before it is reproduced. Whatever changes you choose, you now have a stack of awards to give out, requiring only the filling in of the blanks.

Next, consider who should get an award. One teacher suggested that every child in your class should get an award for something over the school year, even if the award has to be for something like "Neatest Desk of the Week." The teacher can use it for encouragement or to reinforce positive behavior. Still another teacher suggests that you *always* publicize the names of award recipients in your class newsletter, if you have one, in the school newspaper or in the school's public relations vehicle.

Finally, consider giving awards to parents. If you want something super positive, this is it. An award to Mr. and Mrs. Jones for all their help with the class party, the trip, improving their daughter's grades, their understanding and cooperation and/or a host of other reasons that will occur to you, can become a gesture on your part that will reap rewards throughout the school year.

HANDLING SPECIAL GIFTS

A child's teacher is an extremely significant part of that child's life for the year and often for a good time afterward. Of course, we all seek to do special things for the people about whom we care the most. The old cliché of bringing an apple for the teacher might imply a bribe, but more likely it is an expression of affection for the teacher on behalf of the student. Unfortunately, not all gifts given by a student to a teacher are as easy to deal with as a shiny red apple.

First and foremost, whatever your personal philosophy about gifts, no child should ever be made to feel that his or her gift was not acceptable to you. If a gift is given in affection (and any teacher can tell the difference between a gift and a bribe), especially if its wrapping denotes that it is with the approval and perhaps the prodding of the home, it might be wise just accept it with thanks and later write a short thank-you note. Never embarrass a child by refusing a gift.

Sometimes the gift is out of proportion (one teacher received an *expensive* Rolex watch, which, incidentally, the generous first-grade student had taken from his father's bureau) or money (we once got a Christmas card with a $20 inside). Such gifts should be taken to avoid embarrassment and immediately returned in private, possibly with a note or a call home. Be very gentle, but explain that you love *the child* for giving the gift, but it is much too expensive. Do this in private.

If your school has a policy about not accepting money, point that out as well. Your goal in all of this is never, never, *never*, to make the student feel inferior because of a gift given.

One of the best and greatest time-saving procedures is to post your own class policy on gifts at the very beginning of the school year. You can set down exactly what you will or will not allow in terms of gifts between students and/or to the teacher. Anything that does not fit that criteria may then be politely and gently returned in private.

Handle special gifts with special tenderness and care.

GOING TO THAT "SPECIAL" ASSEMBLY

There are assemblies, and then there are *assemblies!* Taking your class to the auditorium to view a film on the benefits of proper nutrition is somehow not quite the same as taking them to see Mysto, the great magician, who has promised to saw the principal in half. The level of excitement and consequently the amount of control you must exercise are understandably not the same.

Let's look at three suggestions for efficiently handling that "special" assembly during your school day.

First, if the children are particularly keyed up and the assembly is not to take place for several hours, amend your lesson plans to do an activity with them that will distract them or divert their energies. As teachers, we are all aware that some lessons and activities can take the full attention of the class and even involve them physically. This would be a good time for such a project. Let them burn off a little of that energy.

Second, honestly appraise whether you will face difficulty conducting your class through the halls to the place of the assembly. If a number of classes are all converging on the auditorium, and your class is particularly excited, you could lose one or two of your charges in the melee, and that is extremely frustrating. If you anticipate this problem, confer with the administration and leave your room two or three minutes before the school is called to the assembly. This tiny bit of lead time can mark the difference between order and frenzy.

Third, preplan how you will be going and where you will sit, and go through a dry run the day before or the morning of the assembly. When everyone knows what they are doing and where they are going, things frequently go much more smoothly than expected.

Here's wishing you a placid trip.

WHEN ACCIDENTS HAPPEN

Accidents may be preventable, but they can never be eliminated entirely. If we could wrap each one of our students in cotton, we still could not keep them from the scrapes and cuts and bruises and scratches that are so much a part of childhood. What's more, we'd discover that one or more of them are allergic to cotton! The point is that accidents happen, and, when they do, we can benefit ourselves as well as our class by being prepared.

For instance, we know of one teacher who never takes her class outside the classroom or to the field behind the school without carrying a small first aid kit in the large bag she carries around during the school day. Indeed, teachers of younger students have learned that playgrounds are natural breeding grounds for all kinds of cuts and minor injuries. In many cases, some first aid before involving the school nurse can prevent infection, and have a calming effect on an upset child.

Another teacher posts procedures for dealing with people who have had accidents and then takes the time to familiarize the students with them, further reinforcing them by a review every so often. When and if an accident happens, students follow these procedures exactly.Finally, be prepared to act quickly in getting aid to an injured student no matter how slight the injury. Of course, if there is a great deal of blood or if the student is lying unconscious or in great pain, send for help to come to you. In the majority of cases, however, you will send the child to a place of medical aid. For almost all of us, that means the school nurse.

Next, we'll look at expedients for getting an injured or sick child to the school nurse in the quickest and most efficient manner possible.

SENDING STUDENTS TO THE NURSE

Perhaps you are in the middle of a class when a student comes up to your desk and shakily asks to go to the school nurse. Of course, no teacher would deny a child access to medical care under any circumstances. What's more, experience has taught us that it had better be quick, lest the child "become ill" all over your desk, which has happened to more than one teacher. So, you stop your lesson and spend the time filling out a pass to the nurse's Office. There surely is a better way.

Indeed, there must be a better way. Even the slightest delay can seem long and drawn out to someone who is feeling ill or has been injured, and we all wish the comfort and well-being of our students.

Figure 10-8 is a Permanent Nurse's Pass. You make this up once out of sturdy material—wood or masonite. Paint or mark on it with indelible marker information pertinent to your class and school. When a trip to the nurse is called for, that pass is ready for immediate use.

If you can arrange with the school nurse to give you confirmation of when your student arrived at the Health Office and/or left to return to class, you can easily pinpoint anyone who may be abusing the liberty. Since virtually all Health Offices are required to keep such time records, this is an easy matter to check.

When sending a student to the nurse, send a student companion along, just in case the first student needs some help along the way. Should something serious happen, the well student is least be able to go for help or contact you.

If any question arises about the welfare of a student, one question sure to be asked is how you handled it and how quickly you reacted. Being prepared and taking every opportunity to see to it that the ill or injured student gets to medical aid as soon and as safely as possible is your surest approach to avoiding criticism.

WORKING WITH COMPUTERS

In our experience, few items in education have met with more resistance or proven more valuable than the computer. We have known some educators who have steadfastly refused to touch a computer until they were convinced of its fantastic ability to save time and be a real help in all the day-to-day workings of the classroom. A computer does not have to be used *only* to calculate the National Debt; it can be used to make up a test or send a personal letter to a parent as well.

If we want to talk about saving time and trouble, then we must talk about using that computer. Many times throughout this book we have suggested time- and trouble-saving strategies involving the use of a computer that have worked extremely well for a host of educators.

Moreover, many publishers are now putting out textbooks and other learning programs that come with a set of floppy disks. These disks might, for instance, contain a pool of questions. At your command, the computer can randomly select the number of questions of your choosing from that pool and print out an instant test that is automatically fair and reflective of the material taught.

What about letters? Basically, teachers keep sending out and using the same *types* of forms and letters over and over again. If those forms and letters (warning letter, missing homework notice, good news letter, problem letter) are entered into a word processing program, then you need do them only *once*. Thereafter, go into the program and change the name of the student or amend one paragraph to reflect the actual situation, and you have a fresh and personalized letter ready to print out. This will take you one-tenth the time it would to sit down and write or type a completely new letter every time you need it.

Of course, we can't speak for you, but anything that can save us up to 50 minutes out of every hour we would normally spend is definitely "user friendly."

THE TEACHER EVALUATION

Once a marking period, once a semester, or even once a school year, every teacher goes through an observation and evaluation of his or her teaching. This, for most educators, is a normal part of school. An administrator or supervisor observes a class; the observer and teacher make an appointment, discuss the written evaluation, along with a friendly suggestion or two, and leave happily. Sad to say, that is not always the usual scenario that is played.

Let us be frank: Sometimes there is enmity in a school, and when it exists between an evaluator and the one evaluated, it is never pleasant.

Therefore, this technique is not for everyone. If you have no trouble with evaluations and can honestly anticipate none, then you can skip this. If you anticipate hostility, however, then a suggestion or two might save you some trouble.

When you are evaluated, go through the class as you normally would. As soon as possible after the class in which you were observed, sit down and, as clearly and honestly as possible, make out the self-evaluation form seen in **Figure 10-9** for that class and that day. Immediately, get your Teacher's Association Representative, inform this person of what you have just done and ask this person to make a note of the time and date when you informed the other. Give this representative a copy of the self-evaluation to hold for you. You can both sign and date the original and the copy.

When it comes time for your evaluation conference, you can legitimately request that the Association Representative go with you. If all goes well, then all is fine. But should one or more points of contention arise, you and the representative have the self-evaluation done within a short time of the evaluator's observation. This document can clarify memories and act as a guide to establish what really happened.

Of course, it would be better if you never had to use a tactic like this, but this is something that is very useful if the need arises.

POST-EVALUATION TEACHER MEMORANDUM

Let us begin by assuming that everything went well with your observation and evaluation. At the postevaluation conference, the administrator or supervisor made suggestions as well as promises of help in certain areas. When you left the meeting, you felt that there had been an amiable understanding had been reached that would improve your teaching situation and benefit your class. Now it is time to make certain that it stays that way.

Please understand, we are not for a moment suggesting that either the teacher or the administrator/supervisor would renege on promises made. We are saying, however, that sometimes the hectic days get in the way of even our best intentions. In short, there is simply so much to do that sometimes . . . we forget.

That is why you might want to try the Postevaluation Memorandum in **Figure 10-10**. In the indicated spaces, place in writing the suggestions, promises, strategies and the like that both of you have agreed on during the postevaluation conference.

What do you do with it, then? Both of you should sign and keep a copy of it. Thereafter, if time gets in the way, either one of you can use it as a gentle reminder to the other as to what has yet to be done. You might want to keep yours paperclipped to the current page of your planbook or attached to your evaluation. It can be a signpost that will guide you on your way to what you want to accomplish.

If both you and the evaluator can view this as an aid to the implementation of the suggestions that have been agreed on, then the Postevaluation Memorandum will indeed have saved a great deal of time and trouble down the road.

Dear Parents/Guardians,

I would really like to give a Holiday Party for your child's class on Friday, December 18. The party would last from 2:30 until 3:05 (end of the regular school day). It would include refreshments (cake and soda/juice), presents (Hanukkah/Christmas), organized games, and general fun for all. I know the children would enjoy it greatly.

I cannot do it alone.

Your help is needed. We need volunteers who will aid and assist with:

Baking   Purchasing Consumables   Setting Up
Decorating   Serving Refreshments   Supervising Games
CLEAN-UP!!!   CLEAN-UP!!!   CLEAN-UP!!!   CLEAN-UP!!!

Can you help? I have to know by December 4 in order to make plans. Won't you help give the class and your child a special "Holiday Treat!"

I look forward to hearing from you soon.

Sincerely,

(Mrs.) Donna Rampino

Figure 10-1
Class Party Note

CLEAN-UP PROCEDURES

I will handle getting the children to the buses and making certain that they have all their materials.

_____ will clean up and "box" any left-over cake and/or soda/juice.

_____ will take down all decorations.

_____ will clean surfaces of desks and tables.

_____ will sweep the classroom floor.

_____ will "bag" all refuse for disposal.

_____ will take refuse to Custodian's Room.

It would be appreciated if everyone would please remain in the room until the classroom is in proper shape for normal class activities.

Thank you!

Figure 10-2
Class Party Clean-up List

VOLUNTEERS NEEDED FOR CLASS PLAY!

Yes, it's that time again, and in about six weeks, your child's class will be presenting a special dramatic presentation as part of the school's annual "TALENT NIGHT!"

As always, we look to you -- our parents -- to help make our part a success. Can you volunteer for any of the following:

Rehearsal Pianist	Assistant Director
Choreography	Stage Manager
Make-Up	Costumes
Props	Scenery

!!!!!!!!SUPERVISION BACKSTAGE!!!!!!!

Please, I know that everybody can help out, and we can work together to make this a memorable experience for your child.

May I hear from you soon?

Figure 10-3
Notice and Needs List

DATE:_____

TO:_____,

   Before bringing an animal on to school grounds, I warrant the following:

   The animal is in good health and has been recently examined by a qualified veterinarian.

   I will keep the animal caged or restrained and will never allow it to roam freely.

   I will personally be with the animal during the entire time.

   I will personally clean up any mess for which the animal is responsible.

   I take full personal responsibility for any liability incurred due to action on the part of the animal.

SIGNATURE:_____
DATE:_____

Figure 10-4
Animal in Classroom Release Form

YOUR NAME:_____

Please answer the following questions as you view the video, "Last Chance."

1. What does Mr. Horton think is Jimmy's problem?

2. Where does Jimmy go when he leaves home?

3. What does Jimmy's friend, Alex, suggest they do?

4. Why does Alex want Jimmy to talk to the old man?

5. How does Alex say he got involved with "Spider"?

6. What does "Spider" want to give Jimmy?

7. What does Jimmy learn about the old man?

8. Where does Jimmy go after he runs away from "Spider"?

9. What is the old man's advice to Jimmy?

10. How has Jimmy's relationship to Mr. Horton changed?

Figure 10-5
Movie/Video Question Sheet

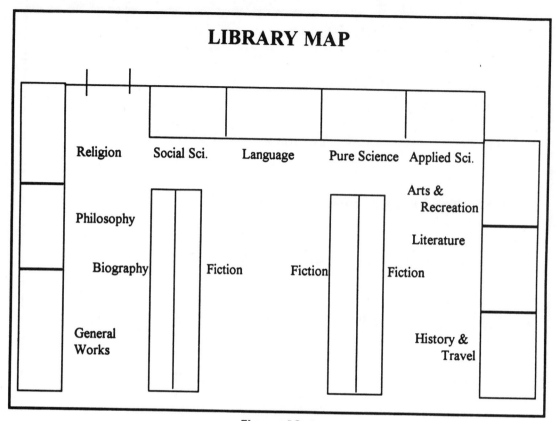

Figure 10-6
Library Map

AWARD

presented to

_____

for

_____

_____

_____

*Date:*_____ *Teacher:*_____

Figure 10-7
All-Purpose Award Form

EMERGENCY PASS
To School Nurse

Teacher: _____   *Room #*_____

(...please return this pass to this Room...)

Figure 10-8
Emergency School Nurse Pass

TEACHER: _____ Date: _____		
SELF-EVALUATION		
Class: _____ Period: _____		
AREA	**SATISFACTORY**	**NEEDS IMPROVEMENT**
Showed competence and knowledge in subject area being covered.		
Exhibited alertness, capability, and emotional readiness to teach.		
Evidenced sense of humor and wholesome attitude in dealing with class.		
Fair and impartial to each child; recognized the dignity of the child.		
Understands and accepts individual differences among students and provides for those differences.		
Showed good control of class.		
Communicates well with parents.		
Contributes to the total functioning of the school.		
Explores and evaluates new approaches to teaching.		
Receptive to reasonable suggestions for improvement.		

Figure 10-9
Teacher Self-Evaluation Form

Teacher:_____

Evaluator:_____

Date of Observation:_____ Date of Conference:_____

Current Date:_____

The following is agreed to by both parties:

SUGGESTION:	IMPLEMENTATION:

Signature of Teacher:_____

Signature of Evaluator:_____

Figure 10-10
Teacher Post-Evaluation Form

INDEX